THE TEN COMMANDMENTS OF YOGA

THE TEN COMMANDMENTS OF YOGA

Paramahamsa Prajnanananda

THE TEN COMMANDMENTS OF YOGA

ISBN 978-3-99000-002-1

Published by:
Prajna Publication
Diefenbachgasse 38/6, A-1150 Vienna

British Library Cataloguing in Publication Data
A catalogue record of this book is available from The British Library

Printed by Sai Towers Publishing, Bangalore.

Dedication

This humble work, *The Ten Commandments of Yoga*, is dedicated to the great masters of yoga from time immemorial through to the present, which includes my beloved Gurudev Paramahamsa Hariharanandaji, who was a great master of Kriya Yoga and taught me the path of spiritual evolution through its practice. I am also offering this book to sincere seekers of truth who have been trying their best to progress on the spiritual path and to reach their goal.

With Love,
Prajnanananda
May 27, 2009

Acknowledgement

The theme of this book was originally drawn from a few discourses presented at a seminar at our Kriya Yoga center in Tattendorf, Austria. In the process of transformation and metamorphosis, the touch of many hands has been felt in the recording, typing, compiling, editing, proofreading, and finally the printing and publishing of this book. Thus, the present form of this book was made possible due to the sincere efforts of many noble souls. I acknowledge their service and am praying to God and masters to bless each one of them.

With Love,
Prajnanananda

Contents

1

Introduction

The title of this book appears interesting. Questions such as the following may arise: "We have heard about the Ten Commandments in the Bible, but is there really anything like the Ten Commandments in yoga? Since the Ten Commandments derive from the Judeo-Christian tradition and thus are related to religion, is yoga then considered a religion?" It is only natural that these questions should arise.

Questions are good as long as they lead to answers or clarification. Unanswered questions may produce confusion and doubt. The word, 'question,' comes from another word meaning 'to quest.' Thus we many conclude that in spiritual life, seeking —quest-ioning— is the best practice. Yoga, as one such practice, is both an art of living and a science of life, which consists of a philosophy of life, a practical science, a set of ethical teachings, and a skillful discipline.

In fact, the word yoga has about thirty-two different meanings. Before delving in detail into our topic, I would like to first introduce the Ten Commandments in the Torah and the New Testament to the reader, or the seeker, who is not well acquainted with them.

While Moses, whom people believed to be the wisest of the wise, was leading the people of Israel from the deserts of Egypt, he climbed to the summit of Mount Sinai alone and received from the Lord a message for the people in the form of the Ten Commandments. This episode occurs in Exodus 20:2–17, and the Ten Commandments are as follows:

1. You shall have no other gods before me.
2. You shall not make for yourself any idol...You shall not bow down to them or worship them.
3. You shall not misuse the name of the Lord your God.
4. Remember the Sabbath day to keep it holy.
5. Honor your father and your mother, so that you may live long in the land the Lord your God is giving you.
6. You shall not murder.
7. You shall not commit adultery.
8. You shall not steal.
9. You shall not give false testimony against your neighbor.
10. You shall not covet your neighbor's house. You shall not covet your neighbor's wife, or his manservant or maidservant, or his ox or donkey, or anything that belongs to your neighbor.

If one studies the life of Jesus in the four gospels of the Bible, one will find the Sermon on the Mount and The Beatitudes (Matthew 5:3–12), which contain the heart of his teachings, given below:

1. Blessed are the poor in spirit, for theirs is the kingdom of heaven.
2. Blessed are those who mourn, for they will be comforted.
3. Blessed are the meek, for they will inherit the earth.
4. Blessed are those who hunger and thirst for righteousness, for they will be filled.
5. Blessed are the merciful, for they will be shown mercy.
6. Blessed are the poor in heart, for they will see God.
7. Blessed are the peacemakers, for they will be called the sons of God.
8. Blessed are those who are persecuted because of righteousness, for theirs is the kingdom of heaven.
9. Blessed are you when people insult you, persecute you, and falsely say all kinds of evil against you because of me.
10. Rejoice and be glad, because great is your reward in heaven, for in the same way they persecuted the prophets who were before you.

Now let us come to yoga. From a thorough examination of yoga it becomes evident, that the practices and principles of yoga have much in common with the Ten Commandments and The Beatitudes just cited. Yet, yoga is neither a religion, nor does it involve any religious beliefs or activities. Although it was revealed in India to great seers, masters, and saints, it has at its core a universal and practical approach which is practiced by people around the globe without any religious or cultural constraints.

2

The Origin and Foundation of Yoga

Let me begin by asking you to pose to yourself a series of questions.

Do you know what you really want? What is the purpose of your life? When you ask yourself these questions, whatever answer you get is the subject matter of the philosophy of life.

The next questions to ask yourself, are: "Can I achieve it? Do I have the strength to achieve what I want?" The answer you get to these questions will be the subject matter for psychology.

Then ask yourself: "What am I doing to achieve the goal?" The answer you get to this question is a practical answer, and is the subject matter of practice.

If you are clear about these three P's (philosophy, psychology, and practice), then you can be successful. Many people begin without knowing what they want. If you know the goal and the way, and you walk with proper preparation, you will reach it. I am not saying that you must study philosophy and psychology formally, but learn enough to be efficient in your own life. Efficiency brings success. Yoga is a subject that requires some exploration of philosophy, psychology, and practice.

Yoga is a philosophy, because it is one of the six classical schools of Indian philosophy. It is also a steppingstone to human psychology, because it deals with the problems of the mind in a very subtle and systematic manner. Yoga is not just a theory, for it calls for regular practice to reap the results of calmness, happiness, and peace in life.

The Foundation of Yoga

Yoga is at present a universally accepted path for living a better life. It transcends religious and national boundaries. The path of yoga, with its origins in Himalayan caves, now unfolds throughout the world. In modern times, people of different religions have borrowed the word 'yoga' and incorporated certain of its principles into their own religious and esoteric practices. For example, we may encounter Tao Yoga and Christian Yoga. Many people simply practice yoga as physical exercises to keep the body fit. However, yoga is a deep and profound subject. Sincere effort is required if one is ultimately to experience the state of bliss that this path promises.

In traditional Indian spiritual practice there are six schools of philosophy. They are: Samkhya, Yoga, Nyaya, Vaisheshika, Purva Mimamsa, and Uttara Mimamsa, which is also known as Vedanta. The oldest is Samkhya Philosophy and the most recent is Vedanta Philosophy, and in between are the four others.

For the purpose of this book, we will explore only the first two schools of philosophy in more detail.

1. Samkhya System of Philosophy

Sage Kapila, who is considered an incarnation of Lord Vishnu, and the son of *rishi* Kardama and Devahuti, developed the system of Samkhya in ancient times and popularized it in India. Ordinarily, the word *samkhya* means 'number.' Therefore, it is said, in such scriptures as the Mahabharata:

samkhyam prakurvate chaiva prakritm cha prachakshate
tattvani cha chaturvimsam tena samkhyam prakirtita

"Since it describes the number, or *samkhya*, which is said to be twenty-four in total, it is therefore known as Samkhya."

This scripture throws light on the beginning and continuation of creation. It manifested as the union of *purusha* and *prakriti*. *Prakriti* consists of twenty-four principles. These are the five elements (earth, water, fire, air, and ether), the ten sense organs, the five subtle elements, and the four inner instruments. The ten sense organs include the five organs of action (a mouth with which to speak, hands for giving and taking, feet for walking, genitals for pleasure and procreation, and the anus for excretion), and the five organs of perception (eyes with which to see, ears for hearing, a nose with which to smell, a tongue with which to taste, and skin to experience the sense of touch). The five subtle elements, or *tanmatras,* are the five sense objects consisting of objects of sight, hearing, smell, taste, and touch. The four inner instruments include the mind to deliberate or think, the intellect to decide, the ego to develop identity, and the memory. Thus *prakriti,* which consists of these twenty-four principles, always keeps on changing. On the other hand, *purusha* is unchangeable. It is the indwelling spirit, immutable and changeless. It is the soul within the body and the creator in the creation. Together, these twenty-five elements constitute creation.

Through the systematic study of Samkhya Philosophy one attains knowledge. Therefore, in the Bhagavad Gita (5:5), Samkhya is treated as knowledge and has the same status as yoga:

> *ekam samkhyam cha yogam cha yah pashyati sa pashyati*
>
> "One who sees yoga and *samkhya* as the same is the real seer."

However, yoga is not a philosophy addressing intellectual understanding only; it is as practical a subject as any branch of science. People consider philosophy and practice as comparable to a lame person and a blind person. Once there was a lame person and a blind person who wanted to visit a festival. The lame person could see but had no ability to move and the blind person was mobile but could not find his way alone. They made a compromise. The lame person would be carried on the shoulders of the blind one, and the lame one would give directions while the blind one carried him. Thus they could travel together.

2. The Origin of Yoga Philosophy

The second oldest philosophy in India is the philosophy of yoga, which dates back to the Vedic period. In systematically studying the Vedas, one will find the principles of yoga described. Yoga philosophy declares that God is the teacher of yoga. In the Bhagavad Gita (4:1), the Lord says, "I taught this yoga to Vivaswan, Vivaswan taught it to Manu, and Manu taught it to Ikshwaku, and in the course of time it was taught to different people in different ways."

Descriptions of yoga are found in the different Upanishads. Among the more than 108 Upanishads, the eleven that are classified as principal, or major, are the Isha, Katha, Kena, Prashna, Taittiriya, Aitareya, Mundaka, Mandukya, Brihadaranyaka, Chandogya, and Shvetashvatara Upanishads. Among these, five Upanishads, namely the Katha, Mundaka, Aitareya, Taittiriya, and Shvetashvetara Upanishads, mention yoga or describe the practice of yoga.

In the Katha Upanishad (1:2:12), it is said, *adhyatma yoga dhigamena devam*, which means that one can reach the divine through the path of yoga and spirituality. In the Shvetashvatara Upanishad (2:13), there is a description of what happens when one begins the practice of yoga. The body will be free of disease, feel physically light, and emit a pleasant odor. There will be a substantial decrease in the quantity of stools and urine, and the physical complexion will be brighter. A lustre and aura will manifest, the voice will be soft and pleasing, and one will be free from greed.

Patanjali's Yoga Sutra

A great sage named Patanjali systematically developed the philosophy of yoga. According to some stories, he was an incarnation of Shesha, the mythological snake on which Lord Vishnu (the sustainer of creation) of the Hindu trinity rests. It is difficult to know the time period in which he lived, or where he lived, but we know that he is older than sage Vyasa and Lord Krishna because there is a commentary by sage Vyasa on the Yoga Sutra of Patanjali, a book written by sage Patanjali. Thus, it seems that the Yoga Sutra of Patanjali is older than the Bhagavad Gita, which is more than 5000 years old. There is a prayer to sage Patanjali that says:

yogena chittasya padena vacham
malam sharirasya cha vaidyakena
yo'pakarotam pravaram muninam
patanjalim pranjaliranatosmi

"With folded hands I give my love and respect to the great sage Patanjali, who presented us with three valuable things: a systematic yoga philosophy to purify the mind, knowledge of grammar with which to speak concisely, and Ayurveda to keep our body healthy and strong."

Sage Patanjali was a master of Ayurveda, grammar, and yoga. This tells us an interesting thing. Each human being has three aspects — the body, mind, and the spirit or soul. We need to develop all three so that the body is strong, healthy, and disease-free; the mind is peaceful, focused, and calm; and we are established in spirit and Truth. This is threefold physical, mental, and spiritual growth. Sage Patanjali was the master of all three, and he wrote three books.

1. Yoga Sutra — aphorisms on yoga.
2. Mahabhasya — a commentary on the Ashtadhyayi, a book of Sanskrit grammar written by another linguist and grammarian named Panini.
3. Ayurveda — a book also known as Charaka Samhita.

The Word Yoga

'Yoga' is a Sanskrit word that is now accepted in English dictionaries as an English word. The word 'yoga,' in Sanskrit, has multiple meanings and uses, some of which are given below:

1. joining, uniting
2. union, junction
3. contact or communication
4. employment or application
5. mode, manner, course, or means
6. consequence
7. yoke
8. a conveyance, vehicle, carriage
9. an armor
10. fitness, propriety, suitability
11. an occupation, work, or business
12. to trick, fraud, or deceive

13. an expedition, plan
14. an endeavor, zeal, or diligence
15. remedy or cure
16. a charm or magic
17. gaining, acquainting, or acquiring
18. the equipment of army
19. fixing or putting in practice
20. a point of view, an argument
21. an occasion, an opportunity
22. a possibility, occurrence
23. wealth, substance
24. a rule or precept
25. dependence, relation
26. etymology or derivation of meanings of words
27. deep and abstract meditation, concentration of mind
28. the system of philosophy propounded by sage Patanjali
29. in arithmetic, addition
30. in astrology, conjunction of stars
31. devotion
32. a spy, a secret agent
33. in Ayurveda, a special combination of different ingredients.

It is not feasible here to discuss each of these meanings, as it would take quite some time. We will, therefore, explore only three of the meanings that pertain to spiritual life.

1. Yoga as a Means to Samadhi

People want to remain in the state of bliss and joy,

but it usually only comes to ordinary people temporarily and does not stay long. The path of yoga allows the practitioner to be in the permanent state of bliss and joy, a state known as *samadhi*. On the path of yoga, *samadhi* is considered to be the goal of life. *Samadhi* is made up of two words — *dhi* meaning 'intellect' and *sama* meaning 'balanced' or 'neutral.' The literal meaning of *samadhi* is being in a state of balanced intellect. *Samadhi* also means being in a state of complete, pure intellect which is free from distractions, and is absorbed in a particular point. *Samadhi* is by no means limited to the states just given, and also encompasses other states of being and experiences.

2. Self-Control

Yoga is both the goal and, as a method of self-control, is also the way. As Jesus said, "I am the way and the truth and the life." (John 14:6) Yoga is the goal; the state of perfection one has to reach. What is the way? The way to reach this goal is through self-control. When the sun's rays falling on a magnifying glass are focused to a point, they can ignite a fire. Our body contains the light of the sun, the soul, but this light is diffused in many directions. If it is focused on a particular point you will receive the light of knowledge and understanding. A river flows down continuously towards the ocean. If we know how to control its flow, we can use the water for irrigation or electricity. If we do not know how to use this beautiful gift of God, it will go untapped. God has given us so much energy and strength, but it is up to us to use them wisely. If we know how to use the body, the mind, and the intellect, knowing the goal or purpose one is pursuing, life becomes more useful, enjoyable, fruitful, and meaningful. This is the second meaning of yoga.

3. Union

The simplest meaning of yoga is 'union.' Union is possible when there are two or more. Our existence itself is the union of the body and the soul. Life only becomes possible because of the union of the body and the soul. Uniting my limited consciousness with cosmic consciousness is also yoga. The union of the bubble with the ocean, or the wave with the ocean, is yoga. Energy manifests through union, just as the union of the bulb and electricity manifests as light. Union is the source of manifestation.

Thus these three meanings of yoga are the goal, the way, and the truth, three terms that are equivalent, respectively, to the philosophy of life, the psychology of life, and the practical knowledge of how to live in this world.

Sage Patanjali divided his book, Yoga Sutra (which consists of 195 sutras) into four parts:

- *samadhi pada* — 51 sutras dealing with the goal and foundation of life;
- *sadhana pada* — 55 sutras of the practice needed to reach the goal;
- *vibhuti pada* — 55 sutras that speak of *siddhis*, or minor benefits, accruing from the practice of yoga;

- *kaivalya pada* — 34 sutras describing the state of perfection.

Have a Clear Goal

When one practices yoga, one gets some *siddhis*, or minor benefits. However, do not stop at these, but proceed steadfastly to your goal.

There is a story of a poor man who earned his living by cutting wood and selling it as firewood. One day he met another man in the forest who advised him to go a little farther into the woods. The woodcutter thought he would follow this advice and went a little farther into the forest, where he came upon a beautiful sandalwood forest. He cut the sandalwood, sold it, and became rich. This continued for some time and then the man thought, "The person who asked me to go farther did not ask me to stop. So let me again go a little farther and see what is there." This time he came upon a silver mine. He mined the silver, sold it, and again increased his wealth. After some more time he thought he would go even farther, and this time he found a gold mine. He became still wealthier. Then he realized that if he had gone all the way in the first place, he would not have wasted so much time and would have been rich instantly and for a longer time.

Let your goal be clear, keep it always in mind, and follow it through to the very end.

The Limbs of Yogas

Yoga has passed through many different stages of development over the course of time. As a result, there are many different types of yoga that derived from its different limbs. Sage Patanjali, in his Yoga Sutra, spoke of the eight limbs of yoga known as Ashtanga Yoga. *Ashta* means 'eight' and *anga* means 'limb.' Here we will explain a little about these different types of yoga.

Ekanga Yoga is the one-limbed yoga: This is the easiest form of yoga, devoid of many intricacies. It has only one limb which is based on the primordial sound *om*. In the Yoga Sutra (Samadhi Pada) there is an elaborate description of *om*. Sutra 1:27 says, *tasya vachakah pranavah*: "*pranava* or *om* represent *ishwara*, or the Supreme Lord." Sutra 1:28 states, *tat japa tat arthavhavanam*, which means that one should chant *om* and contemplate its meaning. It speaks of concentration on the *om* sound with remembrance of its real meaning. In this form of yoga, people begin by loudly chanting *om*, and with continued practice, one concentrates on the constant, continuous *om* sound, which is the divine sound. By listening to the *om* sound, one can go into a deep state of meditation and realization.

Some yogis also consider *hamsa sadhana*, observing the breath as it is exhaled and inhaled by the power of God, with the sounds of *ham* and *sa*, as Ekanga Yoga. Many great masters of yoga, including Lahiri Mahasaya, a great exponent of Kriya Yoga, have also emphasized this practice.

Tryang Yoga is the three-limbed yoga. In the Yoga Sutra there is a description of Kriya Yoga in sutra one of the Sadhana Pada. This sutra states, *tapah svadhyaya ishwara pranidhani kriya yogah. Tapah* (austerity or observing the breath as the oblation in the holy fire in the cranium), *svadhyaya* (the study of the scriptures or the study of oneself), *and ishwara pranidhana* (surrender to God or cultivating the path of devotion) are known as Kriya Yoga. According to this sutra these three practices of *tapah, svadhyaya,* and *ishwara pranidhana* are considered to be Tryang Yoga, or the three-limbed yoga. In this practice of yoga there is a simultaneous integration of action, knowledge, and devotion.

Chaturanga Yoga is the four-limbed yoga, the four limbs being:

- *pratyahara* — withdrawing external awareness into an inner point of concentration;
- *dharana* — practice of the skill of concentration;
- *dhyana* — meditation;
- *samadhi* — realization.

My master, Baba Hariharanandaji, described Kriya Yoga as also including Chaturanga Yoga, the yoga of four limbs, because it emphasizes withdrawal, concentration, meditation, and realization.

Sadanga Yoga is the yoga of six limbs. There are various views in different scriptures with regards to the yoga of six limbs. Here, I will refer to two Upanishads regarding this context.

According to the Amritanada Upanishad (mantra 6):

pratyaharah tatha dhynam pranayamo'tha dharana
tarkah chaiva samadhih cha sadango yoga uchyate

"*Pratyahara* (self-withdrawal), *dhyana* (meditation), *pranayama* (breath control), *dharana* (concentration), *tarka* (logical understanding), and *samadhi* (realization) are the six limbs of yoga."

Tarka, or logical understanding, emphasizes the study of scriptures and accepting the path of yoga as the path of liberation.

In the Dhyanavindu Upanishad (mantra 41), it is said:

asanam prana-samrodhah pratyaharah cha dharana
dhynam samadhih etani yogangani bhavanti shat

"*Asana (postures), prana-samrodhah* (retention of breath), *pratyahara* (self-withdrawal), *dharana* (concentration), *dhyana* (meditation), and *samadhi* (realization) are known as the six limbs of yoga."

Ashtanga Yoga is the yoga of eight limbs. The Yoga Sutra of Patanjali speaks of eight limbs of yoga; namely, *yama* (ethics), *niyama* (principles), *asana* (physical posture), *pranayama* (breath control), *pratyahara* (self-withdrawal), *dharana* (concentration), *dhyana* (meditation), and *samadhi* (realization).

All the forms of yoga discussed above are included in the Yoga Sutra of Patanjali; although sage Patanjali's writings encompassed more than just the eight limbs of yoga.

In modern times, people have acquired many ideas and engage in numerous discussions about yoga. Some think yoga is for making life more pleasant and enjoyable. Others think yoga is done to attain good health, beauty, and some powers. For a few, yoga is the art of attaining perfection and liberation. As we have discussed, yoga is a successful art of living, tried and tested, and confirmed in its efficacy over the long passage of time which has not always been recorded in history.

If we really want to go deep into the subject of yoga, we must know and master the eight limbs to be successful. According to many yogis, the eight limbs of yoga are like the eight steps one has to climb, step by step, to enter the temple of realization. Someone who is strong and healthy may be able to skip a few steps and advance more quickly, but if you do not follow all the steps, there is also a danger of stumbling and falling down. For a smooth climb, it is better to go steadily up, step by step.

According to a few yogis, just as the limbs of the human body exist simultaneously and are interconnected, so the eight limbs of yoga are interconnected and should be practiced simultaneously rather than in succession.

In this book, we will emphasize the first two limbs of yoga *yama* (ethics) and *niyama* (principles) quite extensively. *Yama* and *niyama* are essential aspects of yoga which, if they are neglected, can result in one's downfall in spiritual life.

Kriya Yoga Over time, many types of yoga have evolved. In ancient times, people practiced three forms: *karma* (path of action), *jnana* (path of knowledge), and *bhakti* (path of devotion). These three paths are integrated in the practice of Kriya Yoga, and this has been corroborated by many great masters of yoga. If one studies the Yoga Sutra of Patanjali, the word 'yoga' is used a few times, but without reference to a specific name. The only yoga mentioned by name is Kriya Yoga, and it is mentioned twice in the second part (Sadhana Pada) of this scripture. Karma Yoga, Bhakti Yoga, or Jnana Yoga are not specifically mentioned, nor is any mention made of a yoga by any other name which is currently being practiced today. From this, one can conclude that Patanjali's Yoga Sutra is older than the other yogas; otherwise he surely would have mentioned them. Since he did refer to Kriya Yoga, it must have been in practice before his time.

Yoga is a beneficial path of inner transformation which leads to attaining the state of perfection. It is a complete philosophical, psychological, and practical way of living a richly blessed and meaningful life. The greatest mistake made in human life is not experiencing one's own real identity.

If one knows about one's own nature or identity, then one's life is complete. If one knows that existence is due to the union of body and soul, then life will be more beautiful. Thus, yoga helps us to live a better life. Yoga is the union of individual consciousness with cosmic consciousness. When we are in the body, we look like individuals, but when we know ourselves as the soul, we are free from all our self-imposed limitations as we merge with the Almighty. In every breath, remember who you are and change your life. You should know the Truth, and the Truth will set you free.

3

Ashtanga Yoga: The Eight-Limbed Yoga

Yoga is the art of living and establishing a relationship with God. Yoga is the means by which one can reach divinity in every breath. Yet, the human mind is so confused, disturbed, and undisciplined, that it does not help us to remain on the path to Truth. Everyone knows what truth is, but it is not so easy to live in truth, as the mind moves where it will. Sage Patanjali said there were eight limbs of yoga that need to be followed in order to live a life of discipline.

These eight limbs of yoga are: *yama, niyama, asana, pranayama, pratyahara, dharana, dhyana,* and *samadhi.* Although some of these terms are widely known, we will delve more deeply into all these eight limbs.

1. Yama

There are many meanings of *yama* in Sanskrit. Shandilya Upanishad (1:2) mentions the following:

1. great moral duty
2. an ethical life

3. the first of the eight limbs of yoga
4. God or the lord of death
5. a symbolical expression of the digit number 2.

The simple meaning of *yama* is the lord of death. But who really faces death? A person with knowledge never faces death. Realized persons and divine incarnations never face death. When a person realizes that he is the soul, and that the body will die but he, as an immortal child of God, will not die, who can kill that person? How can that person die? If a person can drink poison from a cup without fear, as Socrates did, where is death? These are examples of the state of immortality. The body is born and the body will die, but one who knows the truth and lives in truth, will always be in truth.

Yama is known as the lord of death in Hindu religious belief. According to belief, just as the soul has determined that the powers of the five senses each perform different tasks, God has designated different powers to different deities. Just as the eyes cannot hear, and the ears cannot see, God has assigned different roles to different divine beings. One cannot do the work of the others since they each have their own area of expertise or field of action. The lord of death, Yama, has a minister or a secretary called Chitragupta. *Chitra* means 'picture' and *gupta* means 'hidden.' Thus, Chitragupta is the one who secretly takes pictures, or records, all of your thoughts, words, and deeds. In the Bible (Psalm 139:1–3) it is written, "O Lord, you have searched me and you know me. You know when I sit and when I rise; you perceive my thoughts from afar. You discern my going out and my lying down; you are familiar with all my ways."

It is a beautiful psalm. When You know everything of me, and are omnipresent, what can I hide from You? We can hide our body from others with clothes, and keep our thoughts from others, but what can we hide from God? Chitragupta takes these pictures and displays them to Lord Yama after your death. Then, Lord Yama will tell you where to go and live. Lord Yama does not punish us, but merely gives back to us the fruits of what we have done. We might forget what we did yesterday, but Chitragupta does not forget. Our life is a life of constant activity. In the Bhagavad Gita (3:5) the Lord said that one cannot be without work for even a single moment.

But what type of work do we do? As human beings we have a beautiful body, powerful senses, a restless mind, varying degrees of intelligence, and a big ego. Because of the soul and breath, all the different aspects of our existence are constantly active, both day and night. We use our bodies to work physically, and our mouths to speak. Sometimes, we speak far too much. Although speech is a necessary means of communication, we nonetheless create restlessness in ourselves due to our constant, unconscious and unnecessary chatter, which creates difficulties in our relationships with people and makes our lives miserable. Our senses kindle within us the desire to enjoy various sense objects, and as a result, both body and mind become tired, agitated, and sick. While we often apply our intelligence creatively, it can be used in the wrong way, bringing destruction to us all. Above all, because of our ego, we see ourselves as the person performing the actions, and claim for ourselves the fruit of those actions, which leads to our bondage.

The meaning of *yama*, as related to yoga, is discipline. As mentioned previously, yoga is a way of life. Yoga is not just keeping your eyes closed and going within, but also keeping your eyes wide open and living in the world consciously. Yoga teaches us how to live in the world, and *yama* is the discipline that trains us how to live in the world. It teaches us about our relationship with others and how to interact with them, as well as how to live with love and a divine purpose. We will come back to *yama* in detail later, for now remember that *yama* teaches us the way of self-discipline.

2. Niyama

The simple translation of *niyama* is 'rules.' The principles and rules that I establish for myself on how to live are *niyama*. So from *yama*, which covers our relationship with others and how to live with them, we come to *niyama*, which shows us how to live with ourselves. Through *niyama*, one follows certain rules in one's own personal life and establishes a relationship with one's body and the senses. While *yama* is about the relationship we have with others, *niyama* is about the relationship we have to our bodies and our senses. What is the body? What are the senses? How will I use them? This is what is explained in *niyama*.

Now it becomes even more internal. I know my body and my five sense organs, and I know that I want to keep them under my control. My life is one of many activities and there are protocols and rules of conduct that need to be followed. The way I use my body to brush my teeth is different from the way I eat food. The way I sit in the bathtub is different from the way I sit in the dining room. The clothes I wear to work are different from the ones I wear to sleep. In all aspects of life there are commonly accepted ways of doing things.

The different meanings of *niyama* in Sanskrit are:

1. restricting, checking
2. taming, subduing
3. rule, precept, or law
4. necessity or obligation
5. an agreement
6. any voluntary or self-imposed disciplines
7. the second limb of Ashtanga Yoga, restraint of mind
8. keeping down or lowering
9. effort
10. any minor observance

3. Asana

Asana is translated as 'posture.' From the time we get up in the morning until the time we go to bed at night our bodies assume different postures. Movement of the hand while cooking differs from the way you give or take something, and from the way you pray or meditate. It changes in every situation.

A person's natural changes in posture during daily activities are like yoga *asanas*. When a person lies down on a bed, it is like the corpse posture, *shava asana*. When one takes a shower, the standing posture is *tada asana*. When one takes a bath, it is like the boat posture, *nava asana*. When one is sitting on a chair, it is another posture, and when one is bending down to lift up an object, it is yet another physical *asana*.

Yogis developed a system of disciplining the body with the *asanas*. It is said that there are as many *asanas* as there are species in the world. According to Vedic culture, there are 8.4 million species, which equates to 8.4 million *asanas*. But to make the system simpler they reduced the number of *asanas* to 84. From these, they recommended a few postures to be done to cultivate a spiritual life and develop a strong and healthy body that can again be divided into three categories. These are *asana, bandha,* and *mudra*.

Sage Patanjali described or defined *asana* as *sthiram sukham asanam:* "The posture one uses should be steady and comfortable." For meditation and in our spiritual life we have to keep our legs and hands in a comfortable position to avoid unnecessary movement without purpose. According to the teaching of Lord Buddha, in the Dhammapada, if you cannot keep your hands and legs under control, the mind cannot be controlled. Sit in a comfortable way without moving the body or changing positions.

Bandha means contracting or expanding a part of the body purposefully through the breath. When you bring your chin close to your chest and press to contract this part of the body, this is an example of *bandha*.

Mudra refers to a specific posture combined with the retention of the breath while concentrating on particular parts of the body. Those who practice Kriya Yoga are familiar with such *mudras* as *maha mudra, jyoti mudra,* and *khechari mudra.*

Asana, mudra, and bandha are closely related and together constitute the third limb of Ashtanga Yoga. Why do we need to practice these? *Asana* is beneficial when we feel tired and remain idle, because it keeps our body free from idleness and lethargy and helps us to gain control over our physical system. Those who meditate practice *asanas* to keep the body fit and follow the discipline of yoga. *Asana* is easy since it is a physical action that requires bending the body in a particular position.

4. Pranayama

The physical body is the gross body, but the breath is subtler. *Yama* involves the outside world, *niyama* the body and the senses, *asana* the regulation of the body, and finally, *pranayama* involves the breath. From the periphery of the body we are going inwards. Day and night we are breathing and the way we breathe changes throughout the day. When we lie down we have one type of breath, and when we work we have another type of breath. Our breath changes with every action and does so without our being aware of it. The changes of breath with our activities are natural, and most of the time, our breath is more externalized. In this condition one can feel the hot air coming out of the nose with a great deal of force. When one is angry, hot air as breath can be felt outside the nose for quite a distance. According to the yogis, the angry breath can be measured as thirty-two fingers wide outside the nose. We consume more *prana*, or life energy, when we are angry which leaves us feeling quite depleted. Yogis advise us to reduce the length of the external breath and internalize it. When you inhale fresh air with long, slow, deep breaths, and exhale slowly and rhythmically, you do not exhale hot air. The distance that the breath travels from the nostrils will not be as far.

Pranayama is a scientific way of regulating the breath to regulate life. Many types of *pranayama* are used for different purposes. In spiritual life, *pranayama* regulates the breath, and many teachers of Kriya Yoga, including Paramahamsa Hariharananda, have maintained that the breath and the mind are correlated. By transforming our breath we can transform our mind. *Pranayama* removes the rajasic and tamasic qualities from us. Tamasic qualities produce *alasya* (laziness) and *pramada* (confusion or doubt), causing lethargy, and rajasic qualities make us restless and active externally. By eliminating the tamasic and rajasic qualities through *pranayama*, one can make both body and mind more sattvic, or peaceful, loving, and brilliant.

5. Pratyahara

Pratyahara means 'withdrawal.' What is it that we are withdrawing? Life energy manifests throughout the body. Suppose a lamp is covered with a basket that has nine holes. Light from the inside will escape through the nine holes. Our body is like this basket, the nine holes being our eyes, ears, mouth, and so on. The light which goes out through every sense organ draws us out into the external world since every door of our body is open to the outside world. In yoga one is taught to withdraw from the outside and go inside, so one can emerge with new light, new love, and new understanding. Yoga is positive living with love and understanding. So, withdraw and go inside. As the mind tries to go outwards again and again, keep reining it back in. An example is given in the Bhagavad Gita (2:58): "Just as the tortoise withdraws its limbs into its shell when it apprehends danger, we should withdraw our outwardly focused minds."

6. Dharana

The five practices discussed so far are external limbs of yoga. The next three are internal limbs. The simple meaning of *dharana* is 'concentration.' In the Yoga Sutra of Patanjali, *dharana* is defined as *deha bandha chaitanya dharana:* "To keep your mind focused on one part of the body." *Dharana* involves closing the eyes and concentrating, while keeping the mind focused on a particular part of the body. Where do you keep your concentration? Some say concentrate on the navel, some say the heart. Some say the heart is on the left and some say it is on the right. Some recommend keeping one's concentration at the midpoint of the eyebrows, while others say it should be the fontanel. Concentrate on any part with which you feel comfortable.

7. Dhyana

Dhyana means 'meditation.' *Dhyana* involves repeatedly bringing the mind back to the focus of concentration. When you continue to practice in this way, your concentration will remain absorbed on that point for increasingly longer periods of time. Eventually, there will be no play of the mind, which will remain still. Gurudev Paramahamsa Hariharananda used to say: *dhyana samlína manasa:* "meditation is the dissolution of the mind." It can also be put another way: *dhyanam nirvisayam manaha:* "the mind is free from thoughts during *dhyana.*"

8. Samadhi

Samadhi is the eighth and last limb, the ultimate attainment of the practice of yoga. It can be compared to a tree producing ripe fruit. *Samadhi* is the fruit of a yogic lifestyle. As meditation becomes more developed, one experiences the bliss of *samadhi.* In the Yoga Sutra of Patanjali there is an elaborate description of different stages of *samadhi.* (For a detailed study one can refer to the Samadhi Pada sutras 41, 43, 44, 45, 46, 47, 48.)

These eight limbs of yoga can be divided into two groups. *Yama, niyama, asana,* and *pranayama* form one group; with *pratyahara, dharana, dhyana,* and *samadhi* forming the second. The first four are related more to one's body and way of being in the world, while the last four relate more to inner awareness. This is the reason for many advanced yogis following only the last four, since the ultimate objective on the path of yoga is realization. However, the general practitioner of yoga should not neglect any of the external and internal practices.

These eight limbs of yoga help us to develop our lives, bringing us success and a sense of purpose. Once you go up the steps, you come back in the same gradual way in a joyful loving state with a new relationship to your body and mind. In Sadhana Pada (sutra 28), it is said that if you practice the limbs of yoga, you will be free from all impurities and experience the manifestation of the fire of knowledge, and will also become well-established in the state of discrimination and liberation. Yoga is a philosophy of life, a psychology of life, as well as a practical aspect of life. Utilize every moment in a conscious, intelligent way, doing all the activities as an offering to God.

4

The Ten Commandments

Human life is a gift of God. Since appearing in a human body is such a rare event, the body is considered to be a temple. In the Bible (1 Corinthians 6:19), it is said: "Do you not know that your body is a temple of the Holy Spirit, who is in you, whom you have received from God?" Not only is your body a holy temple, but each and every human body is a temple of the Divine. When the experience of this awareness expands, one perceives the entire universe as the temple of God, as well. We visit various temples, mosques, churches, and synagogues to chant, sing, pray and meditate, so that we can feel the presence of God. Just as you feel the presence of God when you enter a temple, you should feel the presence of God inside the temple of your own body, as well as in the entire universe, which is God's temple.

Yoga, which perfects the art of living, helps us to discipline our lives, and even changes our attitude towards others and the entire universe, to one of love and compassion. When we are in the world, we live both as individuals as well as part of a community, so we should respect others as an integral part of our own existence. Whether we know it or not, we are always directly or indirectly dependent on the help of others. Life can never be completely personal or self-centered. We influence the lives of others, just as we are influenced by the lives of others. Human life gives us the opportunity to live a life of healthy relationships and positive interactions, not just with human beings, but also with all other life forms in the world. Yoga systemically teaches us how to live with others with a positive outlook and loving spirit.

In the second book of the Yoga Sutra of Patanjali, Sadhana Pada, from sutra 29 onwards, an elaborate description of each of the eight limbs is given. Now that we have some knowledge about the eight limbs, we will look more closely at the first two limbs — *yama* and *niyama,* which each contain five steps. *Yama* and *niyama* are extensively discussed in sutras 30 to 45 in Sadhana Pada. These two limbs provide guidelines on how to behave with others and how to be within oneself. Under the limb of *yama* there are five ethical values to be cultivated, and in the practice of *niyama* there are five inner practices, thus totaling ten. Taken together, these ten ethical and moral practices bring goodness, truth, and beauty to a person's life, and are known as the "Ten Commandments" of yoga.

5

Yama and Niyama: The Path of Self-Discipline

Yama, Ethical Living

Yama teaches us how to live in the world in a disciplined way, so that we can relate to others with love and self-control. There are five disciplines in *yama* — *ahimsa, satya, asteya, brahmacharya,* and *aparigraha,* which are described in Sadhana Pada (sutra 30).

1. *Ahimsa* is the practice of nonviolence, non-injury, and not killing or hurting others.
2. *Satya* is being truthful.
3. *Asteya* is refraining from stealing, or taking what is not freely given.
4. *Brahmacharya* means celibacy, continence, or self-control.
5. *Aparigraha* is the principle of not accepting gifts from others.

These are the five *yamas* of the Yoga Sutra of Patanjali. After describing these five, the *rishi* immediately added that these five principles are vital for everyone.

> *jati desha kala samaya anavacchinnah sarvabhauma mahavratam*
>
> —*Sadhana Pada (sutra 31)*

> "These go beyond race or place, or particular periods of time; these are universal values which transcend all limitations."

Many people think that yoga is a part of Hinduism, but this is incorrect. Yoga is a universal way of life. It does not require you to change your belief or religion. It does, however, strengthen your faith and religious belief.

The *rishi's* word, *sarvabhauma,* means 'universal,' and *mahavrata* means 'the great principles to be applied in your life.' *Jati* in Sanskrit has multiple meanings and can refer to one's birth, caste, race or family, a class or genus (such as animals or plants), and sometimes it is also used for gender. While explaining the concept of *jati,* many scholars dogmatically speak about the word 'caste.' The caste system, in some form, has existed in India from time immemorial. Some people mistakenly think that these values or ethical principles are only meant to be followed by *Brahmins,* priests, or monks. Yet, sage Patanjali made it quite clear in sutra 31 that these principles are to be followed by all of humanity.

Holy places and places of pilgrimage are called *desha.* People usually follow some disciplines while on a pilgrimage or when in a holy place. *Desha* can also refer to a country. By stating that they are not limited to *desha*, sage Patanjali makes it abundantly clear that these principles are to be followed in daily life by everyone.

Kala refers to an auspicious or significant time, such as Christmas for Christians, or Ramadan for Muslims. During these special times, people follow such disciplines as not telling lies or hurting others, and being kind and generous to one's fellow man. Because these *yamas* are said to be beyond *kala* (time), they are not limited to a particular place and time, but should be observed at all times and in all places.

Niyama

Niyama is the second limb of yoga which comprises five *niyamas*, or principles. These are described by sage Patanjali in sutra 32 of Sadhana Pada, and are to be consistently and faithfully practiced by the seeker. In essence, these principles show us how to achieve inner transformation. While this is always related to one's own being, it will naturally have an effect on others. The five *niyamas* are:

1. *shaucha* — refers to purity
2. *santosha* — means contentment
3. *tapah* — translated as self-mortification, is to accept things without complaint
4. *svadhyaya* — is study
5. *ishwara pranidhana* — is to love God, to surrender and make offerings to God, or to accept God.

The ten commandments of yoga, consisting of the five aspects of *yama* and the five aspects of *niyama*, are the fundamentals on which the success of yoga depends.

6

Ahimsa: A Life of Doing No Harm

The First Commandment

What is *ahimsa? A* means 'negation' or 'no' and *himsa* means 'to hurt.' To hurt or kill another, to think or speak badly about others, and to create bad feelings in the minds or hearts of others, are all part of *himsa,* and *ahimsa* is the negation of all of these.

We are part of a family, a society, a country, and a world at large. How do I live, and what type of relationship do I have with others? How do I speak to and behave towards others? Instead of being the protectors of the world, human beings are becoming the destroyers of God's creation. Most religions speak of *ahimsa.* In the Ten Commandments of Moses you find the injunction, "Do not kill others." Jesus teaches lessons about love and not hurting others on every page of the New Testament. The Quran has similar teachings, and Buddhism is completely based on nonviolence. All religions speak of *ahimsa,* yet in practice, what do we do? Yoga teaches us that *ahimsa* should be practiced as a universal value of life.

If we are practical in our thinking, we realize that even when we are breathing, we are killing some forms of life. When we walk, we inadvertently step on some insects and kill them. While cooking, we kill some forms of life with the heat of the stove. How then can we practice nonviolence? This is a basic question. Some violence is unavoidable and cannot be helped. Do not worry about these things, but be mindful of that which can be avoided. *Ahimsa* can be of three types: mental, verbal, and active.

Mental Ahimsa

At the mental level, *ahimsa* would include the following principles: I will not think badly of others. In my relationship with others, I will refrain from entertaining thoughts of anger, aggression, or jealousy. Is this possible? It is possible, but it will take some time. First, be sure that you have the desire to do this. Because sage Patanjali said it is a universal principle, it has to be possible to follow and practice it. Yogis have experienced that when they cultivate *ahimsa*, even animals that are ferocious in nature could lose their ferocity in their presence.

Verbal Ahimsa

Through my speech I will not harm others, nor will my words create anger or jealousy. Political parties tend to create jealousy and hatred against the other party. Social groups and nations use language to create strife. Sometimes, even family members engage in this behavior. It is common in the West that when parents are separated or divorced, one parent speaks against the other parent to the child. Unfortunately, they are not taking into consideration their influence on the children, and that they are filling their heads with harmful and negative ideas at a very tender age. Regrettably, harmful speech is a widespread practice which happens all over the world.

Ahimsa in Action and Behavior

Examining action and behavior is such a vast subject requiring much discussion and debate. It covers the association of the food we eat and whether it is with violence or nonviolence — a question of being vegetarian or non-vegetarian. It is for you to decide. Don't try to find a universal answer. Begin with yourself and see what is good for you. It is a personal choice. Out of temptation people do many wrong things. George Bernard Shaw was a vegetarian. He once said, "I do not want to make my stomach a graveyard of dead animals." When Mahatma Gandhi was very young a friend influenced him. The friend argued that the British were non-vegetarians and therefore had more strength to rule the Indians. "If we ate meat," he argued, "we would be strong and able to overthrow the British rule." Believing this, Gandhi made two mistakes. He stole some money from his father's pocket and ate meat purchased with that money. A dream that night brought a turning point in his life. He dreamt that a lamb was crying in his stomach, and from that time onward he decided never to touch meat again. Later, when he went to England to study, it was very hard to be a vegetarian.

Most days, the only food he could eat was bread. However, he did not break his promise. Later he started a vegetarian club where he lived.

We have to think about what type of food we need. It is a choice you have to make. Practice nonviolence in daily life. Do not do anything to hurt others through your speech, behavior, or actions, not even in your interactions with plants, animals, insects, or birds. This is the first step. In the old tradition, planting, harvesting, and cooking fruits and vegetables were accompanied with prayer. Prayer is the expression of your love for others. There is even a tradition in some cultures, that when a house is to be constructed, a prayer is offered to God, and to the insects, and to other living things that are in that soil, so that they will go away, because it would be harmful for them to stay. It is a matter of one's attitude. Exploiting others is also *himsa.* Whatever is unavoidable and inevitable can be done with prayer and love. Cooking should be done with a prayer, and food should also be offered and eaten with a prayer.

To practice *ahimsa* means not to hurt others, not to be angry or jealous, and not to speak with negative emotion. Why not live and speak with love and harmony? The cause for not doing so is ignorance, for we do not recognize the same presence of God in all. If God is in all, how can I be angry with others, or hurt others?

Recognize the Presence of God

There is a story of a teacher who gave a small bird to a student and asked him to kill it when no one was looking. The student thought he would kill it in a closed room. When he went into the room and closed the door, he found that the dove that he had to kill was looking at him, so he thought he would close his eyes and kill it. Suddenly he remembered that the presence of God is everywhere and that God is watching, so he went back to the teacher and explained why he could not kill the bird. The teacher was happy. He said that his intention was not to have the bird killed, but to test the student to see if he understood his teaching, and he was glad that he did.

Let us look at some other aspects of *ahimsa*. When a patient is suffering physically, with intense pain, and without any hope of recovery, some people practice euthanasia to end the person's life. This happened in the life of Gandhiji. He found a calf that was experiencing great suffering with no hope of recovery and he wanted the doctor to give the calf an injection to end the suffering. Is this *himsa* or *ahimsa*? Modern medical science is so complicated. When a doctor has to operate on a patient, and has to use a knife, is it *himsa* or *ahimsa*? You have to think of the practical aspects and the intention behind the actions. Although the doctor appears to be hurting the patient, the operation is performed to relieve the patient and help him regain his health. Whether or not an action can be considered *ahimsa* depends on the intention and purpose of the action.

Pratipaksha Bhavana

Ahimsa is the first commandment of yoga. When

speaking about this subject, sage Patanjali said *pratipaksha bhavana* helps in overcoming negative feelings. Quite simply, it is replacing negative feelings with positive ones. Always keep in mind how negative attitudes hurt our lives and the lives of others. If you study the simple prayer of St. Francis, you will find a similar principle, where negative thoughts are replaced by positive thoughts. For example, he said, "Where there is hatred, let me give love."

There was a monk who was in the habit of going to the river and taking a bath every day. One day a person who did not like him spat on him from a rooftop while he was returning from his bath. Quietly, the monk went back to the river and had another bath and the man again repeated this act. The monk went back a third time without complaint. This went on for a long time and the man got tired of his mischief, and also felt sorry and apologized. The monk said, "I should thank you. I took a vow that I would take a bath in the river 108 times, but I have not been able to find the time for it. Because of you, I could at least take a few more baths today."

When we become angry with someone, we expect the other person to be angry and react, so the drama can continue for some time. If one does not react, how long can the drama continue? When someone is angry, be calm and walk away from the argument.

In India, there lived a holy man whose activities can be compared to those of St. Francis. He always preached nonviolence, not just towards human beings, but also towards animals and insects. His nephew (whom I knew, and who was also an honorable man), while attending the United Nations said, "Last century made the slaves free, this century made the women free, and the next century should see the animals living with their rights respected." We always think of our own rights, but often do not place enough importance on protecting the rights of others.

Help ever, hurt never.

A beautiful summary of *ahimsa* is: "Do not do unto others what you do not want others to do to you, and do unto others what you want others to do to you."

The Three Levels

Ahimsa has to be practiced at three levels:

1. In what you yourself do: your thoughts, speech, and actions.
2. In what you do through others or the work you have done by others.
3. What you approve of.

For example, *himsa* can be of three types. One can directly kill someone, or employ another to kill someone, or approve of a killing. You should not injure anyone physically, nor employ someone else to do it, and you should not approve of someone else doing it. An example closer to home concerns non-vegetarianism, where you can kill the chicken yourself, get someone else to do it, or approve of someone else killing the chicken.

The Reasons for Causing Injury

There tend to be three reasons for causing injury to others. First is greed, the second is anger, and the third is *moha*, or delusion. In India, there is a man who is hiding in a forest who still has not been caught and charged for killing more than 2000 elephants. The police are not able to catch him. Why did he kill the elephants? People kill because of their greed. This is one reason for causing harm. The second reason is due to anger and breeds violence. When we are angry, we hurt others with our words and deeds. Many things can happen when we are angry. The third reason for violence is *moha*, or delusion. This can be seen in many religious practices. Some people mistakenly think that by sacrificing animals, they will go to heaven. Fortunately, this practice is seldom seen nowadays. Greed, anger, and delusion are the three causes of violence.

Perceive Unity

Why can we not live in peace, love, joy, and harmony? There have been many times when I have given the example of accidentally biting our tongue. Even if it hurts, do we get angry at our own teeth for biting our tongue? The tongue and the teeth are one. Harmony and peace are possible when we feel we are one. One who follows the path of nonviolence develops real friendship with others. When one perceives unity with others, the spirit of *ahimsa* is established.

According to the story of Lord Ganesha, one day, as a young boy, he went running to his mother, Parvati, and tried to climb on her back. He found that she was in pain and discovered a fresh injury on her back. He was surprised and asked what had caused it. "You," said his mother. Ganesha said, "I did not do this." Then Parvati said, "You hurt a cat recently." Ganesha said, "Yes, but I did not hurt you." Then the mother said, "Whomever you hurt, the pain comes to me." How is this possible? When someone is in pain, do we feel that pain? If we do, then we have developed compassion and established the relationship of unity.

You might think that this is difficult since there are so many people in pain and question how you could suffer all that pain. Before going into that, first make sure that you are not responsible for creating any pain in others. Do not speak in a harsh way, but speak with love. Do not allow others to be killed or hurt with your knowledge. You should not hurt another, and you should not be a party to someone hurting another. Someone once asked, "If I know that a wrongdoing is taking place which is hurting someone, and I am alone and in a helpless situation, what can I do?" If you are indifferent to what is happening, you are a party to that activity. What can you do? Mentally, disapprove of the activity, and if you can, go and get the help of other people or the police to put a stop to it. Above all, do not merely accept it. Doing whatever you can to help is *ahimsa,* the first commandment of yoga.

The Benefit of Practice

What will happen if you practice *ahimsa*? Sage Patanjali tells us what will happen if you practice *ahimsa* and are established in nonviolence or love:

ahimsa pratisthayam tat sannidhau vaira tyagah
—*Sadhana Pada, (sutra 35)*

"In the presence of such a person enmity cannot exist."

Lions and cows, or peacocks and snakes, which are natural enemies, can live side by side, without enmity. I know a monk in the Himalayas who communicates with peacocks, snakes, and monkeys. When he calls, snakes come. This is a benefit of practicing *ahimsa.*

Live a simple life and try to avoid injury to others as much as possible. Then your life will be beautiful. This is how we want to establish our relationship to our family, friends, society, the universe, and the creation of God.

Our life is a life of love. Creation is a creation of love. Realize the presence of God in every one. Even the person you are angry with has the presence of God, so how can you be angry? Let us not hurt anyone with our thoughts, words, or actions. Let life be filled with love and be transformed through love. Let God free you from negativity and bless you with love.

7

Satyam: The Path of Truthfulness

The Second Commandment

Yoga means bringing about unity. This unity is not just limited to our personal lives. It is through the expansion of our love beyond ourselves and our immediate family and friends, that we experience unity with the external world. We are able to feel this unity with others because we all are essentially one.

What is truth? Truth can be of two types: One is absolute truth, and the other is relative truth.

Absolute Truth

What is absolute truth? Let us look at an example. Many ornaments such as rings, bracelets, chains, or necklaces are made of gold. What is the common factor in all the ornaments? It is the gold. The gold was there before the ornament was made. It exists regardless of whether the ornament is in one piece or is broken or melted down. The gold will always remain, even if its form changes. As such, gold is the "truth" of the ornament. So the ornament is relative, but the gold is absolute.

As we look at our lives, we realize that our bodies are subject to constant change. The baby develops into a youth, then an adult, and eventually an old man or woman. A person's mind is also in a constant state of flux. The only thing that is not changing is you. This becomes evident when you look at statements such as: "I am old. I am young. I am short. I am tall." What is the common factor in all of these statements? It is the "I am" that remains constant. The "I am" is the unchanging part, and is the absolute truth since it is that which does not change.

In the Bible (Exodus 3:14), God said, ""I AM THAT I AM." What part of you does not change? The answer to this question will also be the answer to "Who am I?" This means that you have to know who you are, which is not done by listening to lectures or by reading books. You have to know this through personal experience. If you meditate and gain this knowledge by personal experience, you will be free. Both the soul and love are eternal. God is the eternal and unchanging absolute.

Relative Truth

Relative truth is of two types; firstly, scientific truth and, secondly, the truth we hold ourselves to. At some point in time, you may have thought that the Earth was stationary and the Sun was moving. If someone had said, "You are the one who is moving and not the Sun," you would have said, "But I see the Sun rise and set." From your perspective it is difficult to comprehend that you are moving along with the Earth. At a later point in time you would know that both the Earth and the Sun are moving along within our galaxy. Today's scientific truths may not apply in the future, so they are not the absolute truth.

Another aspect of truth is associated with our behavior, speech, and thought. Since childhood we have been told by our parents and teachers not to tell lies. But have we always spoken the truth? What exactly is a lie? Anything that you say that is different from what you have seen, heard, or felt is a lie. It is quite common for people to stretch the truth or lie.

Speaking Truth

In Vedic scriptures it is said,

satyam bruyat priyam bruyat na bruyat satyam apriyam
priyam cha nanritam bruyat esha dharmah sanatanah

— *Manu Smruti*

> "Speak the truth, speak clearly, and do not speak the truth in a manner that is hurtful. Let your words be helpful and not harmful."

anudvegakaram vakyam satyam priyahitam cha yat
svadhyayabhyasanam chaiva vankmayam tapa uchyate

—*Bhagavad Gita (17:15)*

> "Using words that do not cause any distress or annoyance, that are truthful, agreeable, and beneficial, along with regular study of the scriptures (*svadhyaya*), are called the austerities of speech."

Hurtful Truth

There is a story in the Mahabharata about a beautiful palace constructed by Yudhishthira which was made of crystal and stones. It was an enchanting palace with many illusions and hidden doors, and had the appearance of water where there was none, while there was water in areas that looked dry. Duryodhana, the eldest Kaurava, visited the palace and was fooled by the appearance of water where there was none. He walked carefully; lifting up his clothes, and was later ashamed of having been taken in by the illusion. In another area, which he thought was dry, he walked normally and suddenly slipped and fell. Draupadi, the wife of the Pandavas, spoke and ridiculed him. "O son of the blind king, you are also behaving as if you were blind." The statement was literally true. Duryodhana's father was indeed blind, and his son did behave as if he were blind. However, the tone in which Draupadi said this, as well as the intention of her statement, not only was hurtful, but even became one of the causes of a war. No truth should be spoken so as to inflict pain. Truth and nonviolence are closely associated. If you know that the truth will hurt someone, then it is not a truth that should be spoken. Always be truthful in thought, word, and deed. Yet, remember that being truthful is not always easy.

King Harischandra — A Shining Example

In the Mahabharata there is a story about a noble king named Harischandra. Everyone was happy under his rule, since the king had taken a vow that he would never tell lies and that anyone who approached him with a request would never be turned away empty-handed. Once a *rishi* named Vishwamitra wanted to test the king and came to him. He said, "Harischandra, I have heard that you never turn away anyone that comes to you with a request." The king replied, "Yes, O great sage, what can I do for you?" The sage replied, "Come down from your throne. I want your kingdom." The king came down happily and said, "I will leave the kingdom to you so you can rule." "But wait," said the sage. "According to tradition, when anyone accepts your charity you also have to give them a donation. What will you give me?" The king said he could give him some gold. But the sage reminded him that he does not possess any gold as he had given away his kingdom to him. The king promised to pay him and asked for some time, which the sage granted. With his wife's consent, the king left his wife and son in the house of a rich man to serve him in exchange for money. He took up a job in the cremation grounds on the outskirts of the town to assist the caretaker, and he planned to pay the sage with all their earnings. Many years passed. The queen was serving the rich man, maintaining herself and her son. One day her son died from a snake bite and the queen brought her son's body to the burial ground for cremation. After so many years, the king and the queen did not recognize each other. The queen did not have any money to pay for the cremation and the king refused to do it without being paid, as that would not be honest to his master. On questioning her about her story, he discovered that it was his wife, and it was his son who was dead. At this point, the *rishi* came to them to say that he had only been testing the king and was happy with his commitment to truthfulness. He also granted new life to the prince and gave the kingdom back to the king.

Truth and Nonviolence

Once a *rishi* was suffering in great pain but was not able to die. The king's guards had caught him stealing and the king pronounced the death sentence. What really happened was that a thief who stole the king's treasury was chased by the king's soldiers and the thief threw the treasure close to the meditating *rishi*, and then hid himself. The soldiers, finding the treasure near the *rishi*, suspected him and brought him for sentencing. Now the *rishi*, who was tortured by pain and unable to die, meditated on the lord of death and asked him, "In my life I have not sinned. Why am I being punished in this way?" The lord of death asked him, "You are talking about this life. Do you remember what you did in your past lives?" The *rishi* said, "I remember seven of my past lives and I have not committed any crime in any of them." Then the lord of death said, "In your past life, eight births ago, you were torturing insects by piercing them with sharp needles and watching them suffer. This is your punishment for that." The *rishi* said, "I do not understand. What I did was as a child who did not know it was wrong." The lord of death replied, "Will fire not burn if a child holds a finger over the flames, even if the child doesn't know what will happen?' An agreement was made between the *rishi* and the lord of death, with the lord of death agreeing that mistakes committed by children under the age of four will be excused, so the *rishi* was finally able to leave his body.

This story illustrates the principles of both truthfulness and nonviolence. Do not tell a lie, even as a joke. Those who want to be yogis should always be honest in their behavior. Although we are taught this from childhood, we often do not follow it.

In a Challenging Situation

There is another beautiful story about how we can be truthful and practice nonviolence when faced with a challenging situation. Sometimes it appears that speaking the truth might be harmful to others but, on the other hand, not revealing the truth might save someone's life. In such a situation one might be confused about whether to be truthful or nonviolent. Someone wrote a letter to Mahatma Gandhi that said, "Gandhiji, I will narrate a confusing story. A monk was sitting at a crossroads when he saw a deer run past him in fear. Soon a hunter followed and asked the monk which way the deer had run. In this situation, if the monk told the truth the deer would be killed. If he did not tell the truth, the deer would be saved, but he would be telling a lie. Here is a conflict between truthfulness and nonviolence. What can he do?" Gandhiji's reply was, "You are not required to give an answer. You have a choice of answering or not answering." In another version of this story, the monk said to the hunter, "My eyes saw but they cannot speak, and my mouth can speak, but did not see."

A Matter of Life and Death

There is one exception made in the scriptures, which would allow you to tell a lie, but only under certain conditions. If you can save someone's life, or if many people will benefit, it is permissible to tell a lie. In the Mahabharata, Yudhishthira uttered a falsehood. He said, "Ashwatthama is dead," in a loud voice, and then said, "an elephant" in a low voice. His statement led Drona to believe that his son Ashwatthama was dead, but the truth was that an elephant named Ashwatthama had been killed. On hearing this, Drona gave up fighting and was killed. This was not considered to be a lie on the part of Yudhishthira, as it was the only way to kill Drona, who would otherwise never have been defeated, and consequently, righteousness could never have been established. If it is a matter of life and death, and you cannot remain silent, you are allowed to tell a lie to save a life. However, do not speak in a manner that creates sadness, agitation, or aggression in others, even if you are telling the truth.

Truth can be classified into three types: truth of thought, word, and deed. Do not entertain negative thoughts, but think always about the good, about God, and about love. The mind always likes to think, so allow the mind to dwell more on positive and inspiring things. Do not speak unnecessarily. If you speak a lot, there is a chance that you could wind up saying something wrong or untruthful. When you speak, say only what is useful to others and speak sweetly, slowly, and gently. Do not hurt others with what you say and do. In anything you say or do, ask yourself whether you are being truthful or not. How is this done? It is easy.

Satya Pratistha

In the Yoga Sutra of Patanjali, there are some beautiful words, *satya pratistha,* which mean to be established in truth. What is the significance of these words? In theory, we know that God is omnipresent, since we have heard and read about this. If it is true, what will you see when you look at a tree branch, for instance? To you it is just the branch of a tree, but a true seeker will see the presence of God there. When looking at food, an ordinary mind will think "delicious food," but a spiritual aspirant will see the presence of God in the food. God is Truth. Jesus said, "God is spirit, and his worshipers must worship in spirit and in truth." (John 4:24) God is Truth, and Truth is unchanging and eternal. The presence of God is everywhere. In whatever I see, I will think of God. Using this practice, you will experience God's presence everywhere. If you practiced this diligently, how could you be angry and unhappy? We know a lot of theory, but how many of us sincerely put it into practice?

The Benefit

Satya pratistha is being established in truth. If you practice being established in truth, what will happen? In his Yoga Sutra (Sadhana Pada, sutra 36), sage Patanjali provides an answer:

> *satya pratisthayam kriya phalashrayatvam*
>
> "If one is established in truth, whatever one speaks will come true."

For example, when Jesus said, "Be healed," a healing took place without the help of a doctor or any medicine. If you speak the truth all the time, you will attain a *siddhi* known as *vaksiddhi*, which means that whatever comes from your mouth will come true. This is how Jesus healed people. Whenever Jesus said, "be healed," a healing took place. Those who observe the truth all the time and attain perfection in speech will achieve everything they want.

8

Asteya: Not Stealing

The Third Commandment

While living in the world, we come into contact with many things. Through our disposition, habits, likes and dislikes, we are naturally attracted to various things. Some try to acquire them in a legitimate way, and some try to get these things using unethical practices. Sage Patanjali spoke about the third commandment, which is *asteya*.

Asteya means not stealing. The cause of stealing is greed. Our greed kindles within us the desire to acquire more, causing restlessness in our hearts and minds. We want to possess things, so we either work hard for them, or we try to find easier ways to get them. In modern society all kinds of corruption are to be found, including bribery and cheating.

Asteya means refraining from allowing greed to enter your mind. In the Isha Upanishad (mantra one), it says:

ishavasyam idam sarvam
yat kincha jagatyam jagat

tena tyaktena bhunjitha
ma gridhah kasyasvid dhanam

"All of this — whatever moves in this moving world — is covered by God. Therefore find your enjoyment in renunciation; do not covet what belongs to others."

Different Ways of Stealing

Our minds are often in the habit of stealing. If we see a nice car, we immediately think of wanting one like it. This is also a form of stealing. If a ruler, king, or minister employs strong-arm tactics to collect money, it is also stealing.

Long ago in India, there was a Muslim emperor who was so honest that he considered using government money to earn his livelihood as stealing. He obtained his food and clothing by selling handwritten notes on the Quran, since he refused to use any money that came from the taxes that people had paid, because he saw it as stealing from them. More recently, about thirty-eight years ago, there was a prime minister who was very honest and would not misuse any government property. One day his son was late to leave for school, and his wife asked the driver to drive their son to school. When the minister heard the sound of the car engine starting, he came out and asked the driver where he was going. On hearing the answer he said, "It is the prime minister's car, not his father's car. Let him walk to school. This will also teach him the lesson not to be late for school again." He did not allow the official car to be used for personal activities. This is the ideal one should follow. If a ruler or a minister utilizes public money for personal use, it is stealing.

In business, many people steal. A doctor who prolongs the treatment of a patient to make more money is stealing. An attorney who draws out the proceedings for a longer time just to get more money is stealing. Stealing does not only mean breaking into someone's house and taking their things. We have many things that are given to us as gifts. Our body is a gift, our mind is a gift, our family, society, and education are all gifts given to us, but our greed makes us want to have more and more.

In the animal kingdom some creatures steal. A mouse steals and hoards. In the villages in India during the harvest season you can dig into a mouse hole and find five to ten kilos of rice in the hole. In contrast, birds do not steal and hoard out of greed. Animals generally find and take what they need, but humans show greed. In the Bible (Matthew 8:20), Jesus said, "...birds of the air have nests, but the Son of God has no place to lay his head." Why are we so greedy? It is because of our sense of insecurity. Would you be willing to go to an unknown place without any money? No. Why? Because you have no trust in yourself or in God. We are so insecure that we worry about every little thing.

Cultivate Trust

A man from India was traveling from Japan to America by ship. Before reaching the USA, an American man aboard the ship asked him where he was going.

He said, "America."

"Where in America?"

"Wherever the ship stops."

Then he asked the man, "Do you have any friends there?"

"You are my first American friend," was the reply. The American man was so impressed with the simplicity and honesty of this man that he invited him to his home to stay with him. He came to the USA with no money and no luggage and lived in the USA for three years. How did he do it? He had faith in God and in himself.

Swami Premananda left the ashram of Paramahamsa Yoganandaji without taking a penny from there. He was walking aimlessly when a car stopped next to him and the driver asked him where he was going. He answered he would go wherever the driver would take him. He traveled from California to Baltimore. He then sat down with his eyes closed. People passing by saw him on their way to work. When they were returning from work, he was still there with his eyes closed. Some people stopped to offer him food. In the course of time, he built a beautiful ashram and wrote many books. How was this possible? Because he had trust in God and trust in himself.

Even to this day, there are some monks in India who do not save anything for the next day. If they get something they are happy; if not, they are also happy. If they get more than they need, they distribute it to others.

Taking Without Giving

Society gives to us, so we should give something back to society in a healthy and productive way. What is your contribution to society and your country? People have the capacity to work, but some do not work and prefer to receive money from the government. If you are disabled and cannot work, it is a different matter. If you cannot work, then contribute in another way through meditation, prayer, or some social work that will help to improve society. Taking without giving is stealing.

Ashrams or social organizations are usually funded through donations from the public, and, thus, people who live in these environments are being maintained by public donation. What is the contribution of those who live there? If they live a comfortable life without contributing, it is also a form of stealing.

Using the Belongings of Others Without Permission

In the Mahabharata there is a story about two brothers who were monks living in two different hermitages. One day, one monk went to visit the other, but his brother was not there. The visiting monk, admiring the nice garden, plucked a fruit from a tree and was eating it when his brother came back. When he saw him eating the fruit, his brother told him he was a thief. Quite surprised, the visiting monk asked, "Why? I have not stolen anything." His brother replied, "If you take something from another's property without asking, it is stealing." "But this garden belongs to my brother," said the visiting monk. "You are a monk. You have no brother," said the other. "So what should I do?" asked the visiting monk. "Go to the king and give yourself up," was the reply. So he went to the king and, admitting to his mistake, asked for punishment. The punishment for stealing in those days was cutting off the arms. The king said he would forgive him, but the monk insisted on being punished and came back to the hermitage without arms. According to the story, the visiting monk was told to take a bath in the river, upon which he got back his arms. The message is clear: do not take something from someone's table without permission.

Changing Times

There is another story in the Mahabharata about a poor *Brahmin* who sold his land to another person. The one who had bought the land was preparing the land to build a house on it when he found a pot of treasure buried in the ground. Due to his honesty, he took it back to the *Brahmin* who he thought was the rightful owner. The *Brahmin* refused to take the treasure, saying he sold the land with what was under the ground and so had no claim to it. Since the two could not settle the argument, they both went to the king for his decision. The king asked them to come back later. This incident occurred during the time of Dwapara Yuga, when there was not so much greed in people. But by the time they returned to the king, the period of Kali Yuga (a time of corruption, conflict, and greed) had begun, so they both argued that the money belonged to them. The king said that the money belonged to neither of them, and belonged to the king instead.

As we can see from this story, we are greatly affected by the times in which we live and to overcome the negative influences of these times, we have to struggle to maintain our integrity, love, and honesty, even when the odds are against us; otherwise we can lose everything. Greed only harbors more greed.

Give More Than You Get

Those who are not greedy give to others when they have more than they need, whereas those who are greedy keep it all for themselves. Two hundred years ago there was a king in Punjab named Ranjit Singh. A monk visited the king, and the king showed him his treasury of many precious stones and jewels. The monk asked the king how much use and income the stones gave him. The king said he did not get any profit from them, and that he even had to spend money to keep them well guarded and protected. The monk said, "I have a more valuable stone than all of your stones." The king became curious and wanted to see it. The monk took the king to see a grinding stone and said, "I do not have to spend any money to protect this stone and it grinds the grain to make the flour I need every day for baking my bread."

Your life is successful if you can live honestly with love, and have a smile on your face. If you cannot give anything else to others, you can at least give them a smile. Someone once said to me, "Life can be very difficult, but yours must be a lot easier because you are always smiling." If you have nothing to give, at least give someone a smile and a kind word.

A thief once entered the king's palace with the intention of stealing from the treasury. As he approached, he could hear the king and queen talking about the marriage of their daughter. He heard the king say that he would pick the first person he saw the next day as a groom for his daughter. The thief thought that what he would get by stealing would be nothing in comparison to getting the beautiful princess as a wife and the kingdom along with it, because she was the only heir of the king. So he wanted to be the first one to be seen by the king and he thought it might be best to disguise himself as a monk, because that would give him easy access to the palace. So the king saw him next morning, and bowing down at his feet, asked him to accept his daughter's hand in marriage. The thief then thought that if he could get so much in a few hours just by pretending to be a monk, he could get so much more by really being a monk, so he decided to become a monk.

Three Types of People

There are three types of people in society: those who are thieves, those who are businessmen, and those who are monks. Those who take more from the society than they give are thieves. Those who give and take in an honest way are businessmen. Those who give more and take less are monks. In our lives we should think about how much we take and how much we give, and ask ourselves which category we belong to.

Asteya means not stealing, not coveting other people's possessions, and lack of greed. Some time ago, a disciple was talking about the Islamic way of life, according to which you cannot lend money for interest, and you cannot earn interest on your money, even from a bank. Trust in God, and help others in need. This is a wonderful outlook and attitude. In the Bible (Mark 9:35) it is said, "If anyone wants to be first, he must be the very last, and the servant of all." Those who are greedy will always put themselves first, often at the expense of others. In India, mothers are the last to eat in a family. It is love that can make one forget his or her own needs, putting others before oneself, while greed carries with it the expectation of having one's own needs met first.

The Yoga Sutra (2:37) says:

asteya pratisthayam sarva ratnopasthanam

> "Those who are established in *asteya*, the principle of not stealing and not coveting another's property, will receive a lot without expecting it."

People live with greed and have so many expectations. As a result, their lives are full of activities, restlessness, and dissatisfaction. However, when you cultivate contentment and slowly become free of greed, you will no longer need so many things, and your life will become peaceful and your achievements greater.

Sage Patanjali has said, "Do not covet others' possessions." Being jealous of others' success, or wanting their possessions, is not only immoral, but it won't do you much good. Sage Patanjali is emphatically saying that if you are established in *asteya* or not stealing, you will get a lot, and this is the truth.

9

Brahmacharya: The Divine Road to God

The Fourth Commandment

Every human being passes through different stages of life, from childhood, to youth, to adulthood, and eventually old age. Similarly, in the Vedic way of life, human life was divided into four stages called *ashrama*.

1. *brahmacharya ashrama* — the life of a student incorporating strict discipline
2. *grihastha ashrama* — the life of the householder implementing self-sacrifice
3. *vanaprastha ashrama* — the life of retirement (to the forest) for selfless service
4. *sannyasa ashrama* — the life of renunciation for reaching Self-realization

The foundation of the evolution of an individual was firmly built on the concept of *brahmacharya*. This concept of *brahmacharya* has often been misunderstood. In the Vedic lifestyle, after completion of the first stage, *brahmacharya*, if people did become householders, they chose a life of complete self-discipline and continued this until their last breath.

One can reap the benefits of practicing a *brahmacharya* life regardless of what path they choose to pursue; whether they are a householder, businessman, or a monk.

A *brahmacharya* life requires being disciplined in thoughts, words, and actions. Before you make a promise to someone, think carefully about whether you can actually keep it and whether it is good or not. Once you have given your promise, try to fulfill it with the utmost care and effort. Do not make promises you cannot keep, and try to fulfill whatever you have promised. In practical terms, we often say we will do things that we are unable to do, so think before you commit yourself to something. Do not speak too much from emotion, and do not impose your authority on others. In some countries, dictators take away people's right to freedom of speech. Never take away the freedom of others, because this is also stealing. In the family there must be a relationship of love, not power and authority. While it is good to live freely, too much freedom can become a problem. Too much of anything is not good. If you put too much salt on your food, it will not taste good. If you work too much, you may get sick. If you speak too much, you may inevitably say the wrong thing or speak about irrelevant things. If you think too much, you may become confused or anxious. To bring harmony into your life is yoga. Paramahamsa Yoganandaji said, "Don't work too much, because you may turn into a machine." Do not sit with your eyes closed too much, because although your body may not be moving, your mind will be in a frenzy going in many directions. There should be balance between meditation and right action. To bring balance into daily life is yoga. Always follow the middle way.

Brahmacharya

Brahmacharya literally means a life of complete self-discipline by practicing celibacy or continence. In a yogic text known as the Yoga Yajna Valkya (1:54), it is said:

karmana manasa vacha sarvavasthasu sarvada
sarvatra maithunah tyago brahmacharyam prackshate

> "In every action, thought, and word, and in every stage of life, one who gives up coition is known as *brahmacharya*."

What does this really mean? It can be considered as self-control. God created man and woman to live a self-controlled life of love and harmony.

Grihastha Brahmacharya — Brahmacharya for Householders

Many people eat food, not out of need, but out of greed. They succumb to the taste temptation and eat more than they really need. The same is also true for enjoyment. All too often, we over indulge. Animals often exercise more self-control in eating and mating than we do. The female of a species, especially cows, will only allow mating when the time is right for conception.

Brahmacharya means celibacy, but this does not mean that people should not marry and live together. Married people can also be considered to be *brahmacharis* and *brahmacharinis* if they follow certain principles. In the Vedic scriptures, especially in the law books, there are references to what times are good for the physical union of husband and wife. Manu, who is considered to be the first lawgiver in Vedic culture, similar to Moses in biblical times, outlined the following principles in his law book Manu Smruti (3:50). During a woman's menstrual cycle, the first four days of the period are considered an unhealthy time and are to be avoided. The eleventh and thirteenth days of the cycle are also not advisable. So for these six days, the wife and husband should refrain from sexual relations. The eighth and fourteenth moon, the full moon, the new moon, and when the sun passes from one zodiac to the other, (which would correspond to the twenty-first and twenty-second day of each month in the Western calendar) are also not considered to be good times for sexual union. If a person's birthday, or the anniversary of the death of someone held dear occurs during this period, one should also avoid physical union. The remaining days are permissible. If one wants to have a male child, even numbered days are best, while the other days are considered more suitable for conceiving a female child. There are also some other general restrictions. Daytime is not considered a good time. These considerations are based on astrology, health, hygiene, and many other factors. If a husband and wife who are living together strictly hold themselves to these rules, it is considered to be *brahmacharya.*

The Concept of Marriage

Marriage is a wonderful institution: two people come together to live as wife and husband and to try to live with love and joy. For a successful married life, the goal should be very clear. There should be common interests and appreciation of each other. Rather than criticizing each other, they should help each other to overcome weaknesses, and set aside some time for both to do spiritual practices, and to have children. In married life husbands and wives should keep their minds balanced and regulated between themselves. This is the purpose of marriage, but so often what we see is quite different.

For those who want to dedicate their lives more to meditation and prayer and living in God consciousness, *naisthika brahmacharya,* known as strict *brahmacharya,* or abstinence, is prescribed.

The life of *vanaprastha* and *sannyasa* requires strict observance of *brahmacharya.*

Brahmacharya: To Remain in God Consciousness

The second meaning of *brahmacharya* is to live in God consciousness. *Brahmacharya* consists of two words: *brahma* and *charya. Brahma* means God the Absolute. *Charya* is 'to roam' or 'to walk.' Thus, *brahmacharya* means to live in the world in constant God consciousness. For those who are always in this state, their activities, verbal communication, and mental deliberations will be intensified with devotion and love. This is the true meaning and purpose of *brahmacharya.*

Many people think yoga is a means to enjoying a better life in the outside world. Many think that this enjoyment of life will be increased through breath control and other exercises. However, this is not the real purpose of yoga. The real purpose of yoga is living a God conscious life in every moment.

The Benefit of Self-Control

Sage Patanjali in his Yoga Sutra has described the benefit of self-control in the Sadhana Pada (sutra 38):

> *brahmacharya pratisthayam virya labhah*
>
> "Those who are established in *brahmacharya*, achieve their potential and preserve vital energy."

Virya has multiple meanings in Sanskrit: it can mean strength, vitality, heroic quality, power, efficacy, energy, splendor, dignity, seed, semen, and gold. If one is well-established in celibacy, one attains immense strength, vitality, a good memory, a strong voice, beauty, and confidence. Do not waste your time and energy. Use it where it is necessary in a self-controlled way.

10

Aparigraha: Overcoming Greed

The Fifth Commandment

When people live in society there is a common practice of give and take. We love to receive gifts and presents, yet at the same time it is the custom to give gifts and presents to others. This practice has become a tradition and part of our culture, but often it appears unnecessary and extravagant and also increases greed in people. We possess and store many unnecessary articles, and, ultimately, we misuse the beautiful gifts of nature. Therefore sage Patanjali in this commandment emphasized *aparigraha*, which is defined as non-acceptance.

Aparigraha means not accepting any gift for which one has no real need, and also living a life without possessions or belongings. It is the art of living a simple life. Mahatma Gandhi, a great soul of the modern world, once said that plain living and high thinking should be our motto. When doing one's own work, not depending on others is also *aparigraha*. This means not accepting the service of others unless it is really essential.

In life we need many things, such as food and clothing. Even if you just want to meditate, you will need a blanket or cushion to sit on. So we do need some things, but we should not collect, hoard, expect, or demand things from others. Those who live a life of renunciation should live a simple life and be free from unnecessary expectations and possessions.

The Influence on the One Who Accepts

When someone gives us something, we cannot know how he or she earned the money for it. The impact of the donation on the people who accept the money that was donated is quite strong. When one practices spirituality, the mind becomes very subtle and one can feel the influence of many things very clearly. To illustrate how the things or the money given to us by others can influence us, I will tell a story.

There was a wandering monk who did not have any attachment to belongings. He was always traveling and staying with the people who invited him, accepting their hospitality. Once he stayed with a rich man for a couple of days. On the second day, at midnight, he was awakened by the jingling sound of a bell. Upon waking up to see what was happening, he discovered that the sound came from a small bell that was tied around the neck of a cow that was in the yard. He thought it would be nice to have the bell to use in his worship. The thought became so overpowering that he went out into the yard and took the bell, hiding it in his bag. When he sat down to meditate, his mind was so agitated and restless that, at first, he could not concentrate. As he tried harder, he became focused and realized what he had done. He was ashamed and surprised how he could have done such a thing as stealing, being a monk. He had never done anything like this before. As he searched for an answer for his strange behavior, it occurred to him that it could be the effect of the food he had eaten. He returned the bell to its rightful place and the next morning, as he was leaving, he called the host aside and asked him how he earned his money. The rich man was silent for some time and then confessed that his means were not honest or respectable. Accepting food or gifts that are not earned in the right way, and not prepared with a clean mind, can cause such harmful effects.

In India there are some monks who work hard and do not take anything from anyone. The motto in their ashram reads: "Never accept any charity." If you visit their ashram, they will give you food, but will not take anything from you. If you were to ask them how they earn their money, they would tell you that they work very hard in the garden and on the farm, and publish useful books, which are sold to maintain themselves and also help others.

Greed and Expectation

The concept of *aparigraha* may be understood better if greed is not in your nature and you do not have expectations relating to others. For instance, on special days such as birthdays, weddings, Christmas Day, or New Year's Day people usually expect gifts. If the gifts are not forthcoming, disappointment follows. Try to live a life without expectations. A spiritual person would rather give than receive. Once, Swami Vivekananda said, "Give and never look back. Never expect anything if you have strength in your heart. Everywhere people are so selfish and expect a lot. Where is their love? Whenever there is love, there is only giving."

Love gives and forgives. Selfishness gets and forgets. Don't be full of expectations, but be happy with what you have. If someone is in need, give them what you have. With respect to your own needs, practice a life of discipline and live with a minimum of needs and wants. This will bring you more joy and happiness. Someone once said, "I am like a water tap. I have nothing to give. It comes from somewhere and goes to others." But what has happened in our society? Inequality has manifestly increased. Jesus said, "If you want to be perfect, go, sell your possessions and give to the poor, and you will have treasure in heaven. Then come, follow me." (Matthew 19:21) He was very strict. He also said, "Do not store up for yourselves treasures on earth, where moth and rust destroy, and where thieves break in and steal." (Matthew 6:19; Luke 12:33) What is the use? People try to save and hoard because they don't have trust. There is no end to a rich man's greed, and no end to a poor man's need. While one has countless pieces of clothing, the other has no clothes at all. *Aparigraha* gives us control over our greed, and if one follows this lifestyle, life will become much easier and will allow us to be of more help to others.

The Inner Meaning

Let us now discuss the spiritual meaning of the word *aparigraha. Parigraha* means 'to accept.' We all have had to accept at least a few things. The first thing is our body, which is called *sarira parigraha.* Out of ignorance we think we are the body. We have accepted our body, and have forgotten that we have the body but are not the body. "I am beautiful, I am young, and I am old." All of these beliefs come from ignorance and through accepting the body as the self. *Aparigraha* is an attitude of non-acceptance. What should we not accept? "I will not accept that I am the body. If I am not the body, then the question will arise, "Who am I?" One who leads a life of love and meditation will, through self-enquiry, slowly find the answer to the questions: "Who am I? Where did I come from? Why have I come? What am I doing? Where shall I go?" All of these fundamental questions will arise again and again. By accepting that I am not the body, by leading a life of meditation and self-enquiry, and by trying to live a simple life, you will know the answer to: "Who am I? Where did I come from and where am I going?" This is the benefit of non-acceptance.

If we analyze our daily lives, we will find that we accept so many things that we do not need to. On special occasions, such as birthdays and marriages, people often give us many gifts which we may not really need. Even in our inner life, we can live with limited thoughts, but if we carefully scrutinize our minds, we will find that we have many thoughts and ideas which are unnecessary. We receive many of these thoughts or ideas from others, and we also collect and hold on to many of them.

Possession and Attachment

I knew an old man who used to walk around and pick up anything that he found, which he then kept under his bed. In time, a big heap of garbage would pile up under his bed. His children would clean it up, but he would become unhappy and start collecting again. We collect so many things that may not be very useful. When you possess many things, you have to take care of them all.

I know another person who has a large, beautiful apartment. He goes to work at 7 a.m. and returns at 8 or 9 p.m. just to sleep and shower in the morning. With so little time to spare, he employs someone to clean the apartment. They never see each other and communicate only by exchanging notes left on the table. When you increase your possessions you need more time to protect or maintain those possessions. If your possessions are lost, you will become unhappy because of attachment. To accept means to possess, and your possessions can cause you much discomfort.

Keep Your Needs to a Minimum

How much do you really need? You may have a big house, but how much space do you really need? You may have a big bed, but how much space do you really use? Do not try to possess more than you really need. Try to help others whenever you can. A monk once said, "If one becomes rich by hoarding money, then I am the richest man in the world. Everywhere you look, you can see my property. Whatever treasure is below the earth is also mine. I am the richest of people." Richness is not achieved by hoarding or saving — richness is a state of mind and of being content. Who is poor? It is the one who has the most needs.

Benefits of Aparigraha

What is the effect of being established in *aparigraha*? There is a beautiful reference made in the Yoga Sutra (Sadhana Pada, sutra 39):

> *aparigraha sthairye janma kathantasambodhah*
>
> "If you are well-established in *aparigraha*, you will be able to remember your own past lives clearly."

When your mind is free from greed and the desire for possessions, and it becomes clear through prayer and meditation, you will develop a good memory. Memory is always related to the past. With a healthy memory, you will live a good and happy life. Real memory of the past is to know the cause and the purpose of coming to the earth, which also helps you to be free from worldly bondage. Many people want to experience this, so live a simple, yogic life and you will know about your past. It is a yogic *siddhi* that comes naturally when you meditate. If you are established in *aparigraha*, you will be able to know the past and the future.

The Five Commandments of Yama

The five principles that we have discussed so far are the five commandments of *yama*. They include:

ahimsa — not harming or hurting others;
satya — truthfulness;
asteya — not stealing or coveting the property of others;
brahmacharya — celibacy or continence;
aparigraha — living within your means and not accepting gifts.

These commandments concern the relationship you have with others.

11

Shaucha: The Path of Purity

The Sixth Commandment

It has been said that cleanliness comes first and spirituality comes second. The more people develop spiritually, the more they become clean and pure. This commandment of yoga is known as *shaucha*. *Shaucha* means 'purity' or 'cleanliness.' Ordinarily, cleanliness is external, while purity is more of an internal matter. As human beings we keep ourselves clean by taking a bath, washing our hands, and brushing our teeth. If we did not do this every day, we could contract diseases, and we would smell so bad that others would not like to come close to us. Even animals clean their bodies. You can watch birds as they find water to clean themselves. I have even seen forty to sixty crows take a bath at the same time. Cows clean their calves with their tongues, and cats and dogs do the same with their young.

When I was traveling from Hamburg to Berlin on a snowy, cold winter's day, in December of 1994, we stopped and had lunch on a bench near a lake. Nearby, a woman was walking her dog when it suddenly broke loose and jumped into the icy, cold lake to clean itself. The dog then came running toward me and literally bowed down at my feet. The woman was surprised at the dog's behavior and kept apologizing, saying that the dog had never done this before. The dog seemed to recognize the need for cleanliness before approaching a monk.

You cannot see your face in moving water or when it is muddy, but when the water in a lake is still and clear, you can see your reflection. So the water should be still and it should also be clean. Similarly, it is not possible to see the reflection of God with a restless and unclean mind. A person who is dirty cannot be a yogi. Those who try to follow the path of yoga must follow the path of purity, which can be of two kinds — external and internal.

External Purity or Cleanliness

What is external purity, and how do we put it into practice?

Surroundings — External purity begins with your immediate surroundings, where you live. Your apartment or house, your bed, and your clothes should all be kept clean. This is the first step.

Environment — In recent times levels of pollution have increased because of our lifestyle and the exploitation of natural resources, deforestation, an increase in noxious fumes and greenhouse emissions in the atmosphere, water pollution, and soil degradation. In ancient times yogis lived with nature in an unpolluted environment, which they did their utmost to preserve. Today, we are wasting resources as if there were no tomorrow, and mountains of garbage are piling up. In many developing countries people are not aware of how to handle the excessive amount of plastics which are carelessly thrown here, there, and everywhere. People should be much more conscious of what they use and how they dispose of items.

Your Body — Get up early instead of sleeping in until late in the morning. A yogi's life is not a life of idleness. It is a life of strength, vitality, and energy. Those who linger in bed in the morning remain lazy all day. Get up in the morning with love and think: "This short day is ahead of me, and there are so many things to be done." Time passes away so quickly. A day that is gone never returns. "Night and day, night and day, I look for Thee night and day," Yoganandaji used to sing. We waste far too much time with idle talk and laziness. As soon as you wake up, pray in bed. Let your bed not just be a place of comfort and pleasure alone; let your bed also be a place for prayer and meditation.

Brush your teeth several times each day. Tongue cleaners are now readily available even in the West, so if you can, clean your tongue every day since a lot of toxins accumulate on the tongue. It is good if you can tolerate taking a cold shower. Our body always wants comfort, and if you indulge it by giving it more comfort, your body will need more and more. Your body will benefit from training and discipline. Keep your body clean. If you use oil, first massage the body with oil and then shower. After showering, dry your body with your own hands as much as possible before drying it with a towel. This produces better circulation and better health. In the olden days, clay and water were used for cleaning as there was no soap. Now the clay is polluted, so it can no longer be used. There are alternatives to soap, but they contain chemicals. It is much better to use oil than lotion. Most lotions are made from petroleum products and so oil is better.

Food — Food comes from external sources, so it is considered an external purity. If you really want to be spiritual, be careful about the food you eat. Do not just eat at any time and in any place. If our tongues are not kept under control, our food habits may spiral out of control and wind up costing many lives. If you are not able to control your tongue with regard to your eating and talking, the many hours you sit in meditation with your eyes closed will not be of much help.

Controlling Your Tongue — There is a story about some people who were rowing their boat in the dark throughout the night. In the morning they found that they were still in the same place. This is the same as sitting there with your eyes closed but getting nowhere. The boat had not moved, and they realized that they had not untied the anchor. If we do not change our lifestyle we cannot be yogis. I will give you another example. During programs, I notice that some people eat in between the times set for meals. Whatever I eat, I eat in your presence, and I do not eat anything in my room. As soon as the classes are over, people leave and put something in their mouths. Is this extra snacking really necessary? It is merely succumbing to the temptation of satisfying your taste buds and is evidence of you having no control over your tongue and your mind. What does this achieve? Is this yoga or meditation? Be strict. If you are not strict with yourself, who else will be?

In the Epistle of Paul, he says that he has scolded and given everything of himself and now it is your choice what you want. You have to decide what you want. Some foods irritate the mind, so be careful of that. You eat those foods and then you complain that you are practicing and not getting results. The wrong fuel in the car will not work. Be careful in food and drink.

Do not overeat just because the food tastes good, and do not eat at the wrong time. Fasting can be beneficial once a week or every fortnight.

Cooking Food — Food should be cooked in clean pots and eaten on clean plates. Always cook with love and joy, in a prayerful mood. Do not cook food when you are irritated, angry, or agitated. If you cook with love, it will provide spiritual nourishment for the whole family. Do not overcook food, or cook large amounts, or eat food that has been leftover for two to three days. By repeatedly heating food, the goodness in the food is lost.

Keep food simple. In the West, too much salt is used. Try to keep salt to a minimum, since you do not need it except in summer. Unsalted food provides enough salt for the body. Extra salt only stimulates the mind and puts a strain on the kidneys and heart. In Ayurveda, some foods or combinations of foods are forbidden at various times. If you are preparing any sweets, do not heat honey because cooking honey makes it poisonous. Honey should be added only after cooking. Anything that is sour or acidic should not be put in a metal container. Now and then, eat some bitter food, perhaps some karela or bitter gourd. Although most people like sweet or salty foods, the body needs something bitter now and again. Do not eat too many sweets at night.

After eating food, rinse your mouth, and if you can, brush your teeth. If possible, avoid eating out. You could be putting your health at risk. You can carry food with you if you plan to be away from home for a long time. If this is not possible, eat your food in prayer. When I was young and traveling for months at a time, I never ate out.

Serving Food — Always serve food with love. It is advisable not to eat food from other people's plates, with the exception of mothers and children sharing their food, or eating food from the master's plate. Even if you are close to someone, do not eat half of the food and give the rest away, since it is not hygienic. This does not mean that you do not love them. While cooking food, do not taste the food and then put the same spoon back in the food. Everyone's mouth harbors germs and bacteria, however clean we may be. While serving food, do not let the serving spoon come into contact with your plate and put it back into the bowl again, or scrape food off of the serving spoon with your spoon and put it back in the bowl again.

Drink — Drink plenty of water. Recently, I have seen t-shirts in the USA that say, "No reason, no season, drink three liters of water." However, do not drink water right after eating food. In Ayurveda, it is said, "Water is the antidote to constipation. Water is nectar during food, but poison after food." So wait for thirty minutes after a meal before drinking water. Drinking water in the morning is very good. If you drink a glass of water before eating food, you will eat less. It is better to eat fresh fruits instead of drinking fruit juice.

Digestion — Eat less, chew more, and have set times for eating meals. It is good to eat food when the breath is in the right nostril, since it will not be digested well if it is eaten when the breath is in the left nostril. Now you may well ask, "What if the breath and time of eating cannot be coordinated?" With determination, you can change your breath to the right nostril. A simple yogic technique used to change your breath from the left to the right nostril is to lie on your left side. Your breath will change to the right side in a few minutes.

Maintaining Your Health — If a healthy lifestyle fails to prevent or cure your ailments, you can take medicine as a last resort. To remain free from diseases, exercise or walk fast every day. *Maha mudra* and the bowing technique in Kriya Yoga are beneficial, but walking in fresh air is even better. A healthy body is a pure body, and a healthy mind is a pure mind.

Inner Purity

In the Bible (Matthew 15:11), Jesus said, "What goes into a man's mouth does not make him 'unclean,' but what comes out of his mouth, that is what makes him 'unclean.'" Have you noticed what comes out of your mouth? A string of words. Where do these words come from? From thoughts. Thoughts coming from the mind are expressed externally as words. Be careful of your thoughts and emotions. If you live a simple, prayerful life, your thoughts will be pure. Meditation and good company will help. Keep the mind in a positive and inspired state, and read some uplifting, good books.

How do we benefit? When people live in a clean environment and surroundings, it has a noticeable effect on their bodies, minds, and lives. If you put on clean clothes, you will feel good, but putting on dirty clothes will make you feel uncomfortable. Purity in food not only helps you to enjoy it, but also brings you better health.

The Benefits of Shaucha, Purity or Cleanliness

Sage Patanjali explains in Sadhana Pada the benefits of maintaining purity:

shauchat svanga jugupsa parair asamsargah

(sutra 40)

"As a result of purity, one feels detached or indifferent to one's own body, and does not desire to be in physical contact with others."

sattva shuddhi saumanasya ekagrya indriya jaya atmadarshana yogyatvani cha

(sutra 41)

"In addition, one gains purity of the inner instruments, cheerfulness, increased concentration, control over the senses, and attainment of the ability for Self-realization."

A summary of the benefits described by sage Patanjali appears below.

Detachment Toward One's Own Body

Detaching from your body may not sound like it is a good thing to do, particularly when we are speaking about love and purity. Remember, the scriptures are not meant to be taken literally. They have a hidden meaning.

If you dislike something, would you want to be closer to it? A yogi once compared the body to a big wound and a boil. If you had a large wound, what would you do? You would clean it every day, apply some ointment, put on a bandage, and maybe take some medicine. Sometimes pus and other things may come out of the wound. This is why the yogi compared the body to a large wound or boil, which needs to be cleaned every day. Just as the wound needs ointment, the body needs some oil. It needs a bandage, which are the clothes we put on. There is excretion from all of the doors of the body that has to be cleaned. Our food is like the medicine. If you keep this in mind, you will develop detachment from the body and will think more of the question: "Who am I?" This is *svanga jugupsa* or detachment from one's own body.

This scripture also says that the body is a temple. Just as we clean our house, our body should also be kept clean. The temple's purpose is to be a place of prayer, and the purpose of our body is to realize the soul within, which will also lead to the inquiry of "Who am I?"

No Desire for Close Contact with Other People

It was stated above: *parair asamsargah,* which means "causes concern about contact with others."

To maintain purity of body and mind you have to be very careful about what you come into contact with through the senses. When you see a flower, it is in contact with your eyes. If you just see a flower, you are not a yogi. If you see the beauty of God in the flower, then you are a yogi. If you admire the beauty of your skin and think you are beautiful, then you are not a yogi. Nothing is permanent. See only the presence of God in everything. Life is an opportunity, and we should make the best use of it, yet many miss this opportunity.

There is a beautiful song in Bengali that says:

"I fell down in my own ditch that I myself have dug; no one is responsible for this.

I am in the ditch and crying that I fell inside, but I dug the ditch myself."

We are caught in the web of our own karmas.

Purity of the Inner Instruments

The four inner instruments are the mind, intellect, memory, and ego. Life becomes peaceful and beautiful when they are kept in a healthy condition.

Sattva shuddhi means 'purity in the heart.' Being emotionally balanced helps us to be peaceful and loving. Peace on the face, and love in the heart bring real beauty to a person.

Saumanasa or Cheerfulness

Cheerfulness is a divine quality. The word *saumanasa* comes from *saumana*, which has a double meaning, namely, 'a good mind' and 'a flower.' Just as a flower is beautiful and pure, purity in the mind and heart bring cheerfulness and contentment. If you cultivate purity or cleanliness, you will always feel cheerful and happy. Yet, in the modern world we find so many people with sorrowful and gloomy faces. Swami Vivekananda once said to people with long faces, "Who allowed you to go out with such a clouded, diseased, and sickly face?" Yoganandaji was once traveling by train, and the person sitting across from him had a frown on his face. When Yoganandaji asked for the reason, the person replied, "It is none of your business." Yoganandaji said, "It is, because I have to look at you sitting opposite me. I know your craziness, but you don't know my craziness." Then they started talking. The other person turned out to be a movie star. Yoganandaji told him if one does not tell why he is frowning, then the other person will naturally follow suit and also frown, because people's moods and behavior affect others. Later Yoganandaji said, "I did not have to become a movie star for him to follow me." If you are sad or depressed, close your door and do not go out, since we carry our unhappiness with us into the outside world. If we maintain purity, we will be cheerful and happy.

Increased Concentration

The mind is a great servant, but a very bad master. A disciplined mind helps us to achieve a lot, but an untrained mind only creates chaos in life. Cultivation of purity helps a person gain control over the mind.

Control Over the Senses

Creating and maintaining a natural and healthy atmosphere, practicing self-restraint, and selecting healthy food are the elements of the practice of purity, which gives us control over the senses. In the Katha Upanishad (1:3:3–4), it is said that the senses are like horses, and we are the carriage that is drawn behind them. This is an indication of how powerful they are. Just as trained horses are a great help for people, our disciplined senses become a great support on the path of realization.

Attainment of Self-Realization

In the Katha Upanishad (1:3:8) it is also stated:

yastu vijnanavan bhavati samanaskah sada shuchih

"One who is Self-realized is always pure."

Likewise, purity is the door to realization. Without purity one cannot achieve the state of realization. Outer cleanliness and inner purity enhance the ability of the seeker to behold and experience the truth of life.

12

Santosha: Contentment

The Seventh Commandment

Contentment is a state of mind which keeps people happy with what they have. In this way, they are able to avoid unhappiness and insecurity, and remain peaceful. Contentment is the state of equipoise in every situation. The ordinary human mind is reactive and irritable, and ruins the satisfaction gained from activities and the joy of life. Sage Patanjali is now speaking about the seventh commandment, which is to always be content or satisfied with one's lot in life.

What does it take to make you satisfied or unsatisfied? Try to be satisfied with what you have. However, do not be satisfied with your spiritual practice. Never think that you have meditated enough. How do you go about maintaining a state of balance, and of what benefit is it to you?

In the Bhagavad Gita (12:14) it says:

santusthah satatam yogi

"A yogi is always content."

Discontentment is a human vice that has become quite prevalent in modern times. Even though there is so much material comfort and an increased standard of living, people are still not content. It seems that the more one has, the more one needs. There seems to be no joy or satisfaction. Instead of enjoying a life of peace and contentment, people in the modern, corporate world are not happy. They are not able to enjoy the money they earn, the environment in which they work, or their leisure time, due to stress and insecurity.

Time is life. Time wasted is life wasted. If we waste a single breath, it will be gone forever, never to return. There is a proverb: "Time and tide wait for no one." If we use time in a better way, success will be ours. How can we use time in a better way if our mind is not peaceful and cheerful, and is overburdened with anxieties and worries? If our mind is so stressed, we will not be able to use time effectively. Yoga is a method used to discipline the body and the mind, as well as our lives. It also teaches us how to remain in God consciousness in every breath, and to be content in every situation.

We live in a competitive society in which we always compare ourselves to others. Everyone tries to be bigger and better in trying to outdo the other. Most of our time is used in this way. Whenever I am in an airplane flying at low altitude, just before landing, I look at all the cars and wonder why they are all going so fast. If the cars are running so fast, are the minds of the occupants still? Their minds are not joyful or at peace.

Modern people are so stressed that they do not know how to enjoy life. When people go to work, they think of the weekend when they will be able to relax. So they wind up working hard for five days while thinking of these two days. When the weekend finally comes, there is so little happiness, and sadness soon sets in when the weekend is over. People go though five days of stress and unhappiness with the expectation of two days of happiness, which are often spent sleeping or watching the television. People work all year and look forward to a few weeks' holiday. A whole year of stress for a few weeks of pleasure! A whole life of unhappiness while waiting to get a pension, with the hope that life will be better during the retirement stage. Is this all there is to life? When we do not spend this moment in joy and happiness, it will be wasted. If I am sick for five days, how can I expect to be happy for the next two days? Yoga teaches us to be satisfied with what we have and how to be happy in each moment. With spiritual things, you should never be satisfied, but with material things, you should curb your desires and exercise self-control.

Desire and Dissatisfaction

There is no end to desires. One person was walking and another was riding a bicycle. The one who was walking thought, "If only I had a bicycle, I could have gone much faster and traveled more quickly." So he bought a bicycle, but when he saw someone else driving a scooter, he thought, "Oh, that is a lot more comfortable." So he bought a scooter. Then he saw others driving a car so he purchased a car. Soon, he thought that others had more expensive cars and that his car was too cheap. Is there ever an end to it?

Be Clear About the Goal

A yogi first decides what he needs. Earlier, I asked you to think about what your goal in life is. Ask yourself this question again and again. When your goal is clear, you will work to reach that goal. On the way many things may happen to distract you, but if you remember your goal, nothing will stop you. Often, we do a lot of work, but we are not always sure of our success. Sometimes we may not achieve the desired result, so we feel sad and complain, "I did so much for him, and in the end, he left me," or "I studied so hard, but I still did not pass my exam." Then what happens? We are unhappy, dejected, and depressed.

What does a yogi do?

Accepts the Result

A yogi does his work in God consciousness, and once the work is done, he leaves the result up to God. "Let Him determine what will be, and whatever the result, I know I have done my duty." A yogi is like a successful farmer. The farmer cultivates his land, but he does not know what the weather will be like or how much he will harvest. He must leave the result in God's hands. Regardless of what happens, you should be happy; otherwise you will just waste more time being sad and depressed. Have the attitude that success or failure does not matter. Just do your duty and fulfill your responsibilities as best you can, and maintain a state of balance, contentment, and satisfaction.

Satisfaction and contentment come in two varieties: spiritual and material.

Prakriti or Nature

Prakriti means 'nature,' and controls many things in our lives, such as your digestion after you have eaten, which is entirely beyond your control. So, just allow nature to do its work and let go of any thoughts you may have. I often say that it is the body that is hungry and not you. The hand feeds, not you; the mouth chews, not you; the stomach digests the food, not you; the intestines assimilate the food, not you; and excretion comes out of the body, whether you like it or not.

In the Bhagavad Gita (3:27), it is said:

prakriteh kriyamanani gunaih karmani sarvashah

"*Prakriti* does all the work."

God has determined that our bodies are governed by nature, so different parts of our bodies do their work very efficiently and in an organized way — the eyes see, the ears hear, and the nose smells. Each has its own particular activity.

Even in the outside world, the wind blows, the sun rises, clouds drift by, and the seasons come and go in their own time, following a particular pattern. All of nature is regulated by the presence of the Divine, and nature works within your body in the presence of the soul. You should not be too concerned or worried about what is going on. Do not be identified with your body. If your body is weak, do not think that "I am weak." Your body may be tall, or small, but you are not tall, and you are not small. Always maintaining this type of attitude will bring you contentment, and free you from many worries in life. This is a spiritual attitude, or inner contentment.

Trust

The second type of contentment comes from trust. In India, many monks have an attitude of: "God will take care of every thing and I do not need to do a thing." They won't even go out to collect food, but just sit in one place. If something comes along, it is good, but if it does not, that also is good. Whether or not there is food to eat is all the same. One who develops trust in God is always content.

Time

Time has a strong impact on our lives. When the time is right, something will happen. You have done what you could and not neglected your duty, and now the rest will happen in good time. For everything there is a time and a season, yet we are often quite impatient and cannot wait.

The book that I read most often is the Bhagavad Gita, which I have read more than one thousand times, followed by the Bible. I also like the book *Siddhartha* and have read it at least twenty-five times in my life, even though it is not more than one hundred pages long. In this book, *Siddhartha*, it says: "I know three things: how to wait, how to think, and how to fast." I was very young when I first read this book and thought that if he could have these three qualities, then so could I. To be able to wait for the right time to come is important. There is a time for everything. A plant grows in time, flowers bloom in time, and fruit grows in time. If a plant were to grow overnight, it would be unnatural. So, as we have seen, the influence of time is the third spiritual factor.

Destiny

The fourth spiritual factor is destiny. Do not think that destiny is something that is imposed on you, that God has given each of us a different destiny. We create our own destiny. Destiny is nothing but the result of our own past actions, some of which we may have long forgotten. However, many things we do bring an instant result. You may be hungry, so you go and eat something, and then you are satisfied. This is an instant result. I smiled and you smiled back. This is also an instant result, but some results take a bit more time. A student going to medical school will have to work hard and do a lot of study for many years before becoming a doctor. Then, there is the little girl who wants to be a mother; how many years does that take? With so many things we do in life, there is a great deal of time that passes between the action we take, and the awaited result. Many karmas result from actions taken a very long time ago, and consequently we do not remember them.

Many unknown factors influence our destiny and are the result of our own past karma. In my own case, when I was a young boy, I went through so much suffering and disease. Why? I might have thought that I had not done anything in this life to deserve this, because I had suffered right from birth. Is God unjust?

Why did He give so much suffering to me? This is where destiny comes in. There is so much past karma that is having an influence on me, but I should not become a slave of destiny. If I have touched something dirty, my hand will be dirty, but then it should be cleaned. With positive effort and a prayerful attitude, we can change our destiny.

A yogi accepts these four factors in cultivating inner contentment. God is there, and has sent me to this world. God has given me a human birth, a good brain, and even some skills and talents, which I will use in a positive, purposeful, productive way. This attitude will bring a state of inner contentment that will remain with us throughout our lives, no matter what happens.

Accept the Inevitable

There once was a very rich man who had an import-export business. One day he decided to invest all of his money and quit the business, happy to receive whatever return he would get. All his family members wanted to board the ship before it sailed, since it was to be the last trip. Everyone went, except this man. Sometime later, a servant came to him with a message and said, "Master. I have sad news."

"What is the news?" asked the man.

"The ship sank in the ocean."

"What?" asked the man."

"The ship sank. You lost all your property and everything you invested. You lost all your family members."

"So what. That's just the way life is," said the man. Look at his response. He had just lost everything, his material possessions, his family, and his status. His initial response, "What?" was a statement of disbelief and his second response, "So what. That's just the way life is," was one of acceptance. Initially, he could not believe what had happened, but in the next moment, he accepted the truth. Whatever you cannot change, accept it with a smile or a tear, but even if you cry for years and years, it will not change anything. If I have lost a near and dear one, will crying bring her back to me? To accept the truth with inner contentment and a smile is a better way of life, but there are very few who have the courage to accept the truth with a smile. We cry and expect others to share our sadness and console us, and we complain if they do not come in our time of need. A yogi is always content in the material life, but is never content in spiritual life, since he always wants more.

While living in the world, we need many things and acquire a lot of possessions. Although many people spend a lot of time accumulating things, they do not know what to do with them afterwards. It creates big problems in life. People are not ready to give up their things, nor do they know what to do with them. However, if you do not know how to use what you have, what will you do with it? If you had a million dollars, what would you do with the money? Protecting your wealth can also be arduous. A big house is harder to maintain than a smaller one. If you lose something, it causes you pain, and when something of yours is used or enjoyed by others it also gives you pain. A yogi remembers the pain associated with possessions, so a yogi is content with what he has.

The Benefit of Contentment

What will happen if you are always content with what you have? In the Yoga Sutra of Patanjali (Sadhana Pada, sutra 42), it says:

santoshad anuttamah sukha labhah

"If you are established in contentment, you will always experience superlative happiness."

Do you want to be happy or not? To secure happiness tomorrow, would you cry today?

There is a story about a man who wanted to know how the construction of a temple was going, so he went there and greeted the first man he met, asking "How are you?"

"Don't even ask. I'm working hard from dawn until dusk. The king wants the temple to be completed at a set time, so I have no time to sleep. Even if I worked forty-eight hours a day, I would not be able to complete it," replied the man. The questioner went to another man and asked the same question. The second man replied, "I'm doing well. I need money, because my wife is sick. With the money I earn here, I will be able to take her to the hospital. Anyhow, I am earning money." A third man who was asked the same question said, "I am very happy. I am building this floor, stone after stone, and can imagine what the temple will look like. Each stone is laid with so much love. The people will be walking on each of these stones to go to the altar and pray. It is a great opportunity. How many people will get this chance in life?" All three of these people were doing the same work, but each had a completely different attitude. For each of them, the results will also be different. With what attitude do we work?

One who regularly maintains contentment for longer periods of time will experience *anupama sukha* (happiness beyond comparison). So be content. How can you be content? By not having expectations, by trusting in God with the knowledge that He provides everything.

God Provides

There is a story of a young monk who lived in a monastery his entire life. He went out into the world to go begging for the first time after receiving permission from his master. As he stood in front of a house, a young woman came out to give him food. Not having seen a member of the opposite gender before, the monk innocently asked, "Do you have a health problem? Are those tumors or boils on your chest?" The young woman was scared and went inside the house and told her mother-in-law what happened. The mother-in-law came out and immediately understanding the problem, explained to the young monk that God had given women milk in their breasts to feed a newborn child. The monk said, "Thank you," and was about to leave. The woman was surprised and asked, "Don't you want the food?"

He replied, "If God has provided food for a baby even before it is born, will He not provide for me without having to go from door to door?" This monk accepted prayer and meditation as his way of life, renouncing anything else. We should always do our duty as an offering to God and leave the rest in the hands of God. Practice acceptance. If you think something better could be done, by all means do so, but do not allow tension or worry to cloud your heart. Prayerful and conscious living will help you to control your emotions.

13

Tapah: The Path of Inner Discipline

The Eighth Commandment

There is no substitute for hard work. When Self-realization or spiritual growth is considered the highest goal in spiritual achievement, it naturally requires continuous sincere effort. Sage Patanjali, while describing inner development and transformation, emphasized *tapah*. In his Yoga Sutra, he has mentioned *tapah* several times.

What does *tapah* mean? It has multiple meanings, among them, heat or fire, religious austerity, pain or suffering, meditation connected with the practice of physical mortification, or special observances. *Tapah* is the practice of doing difficult things to mortify the body for the purpose of discipline and tolerance. Some people sit with their hands up in the air and meditate for long periods of time. Others sit around a fire in summer and meditate, or stand in cold water in winter and torture the body in pursuit of their goal

The second aspect of *tapah* comes from the root word *tapa*, meaning 'temperature.' Each body maintains its temperature, which is done through circulation and the breath. The temperature of the body is maintained through conscious breathing, which is *tapah.*

Tapah can also be the ability to tolerate hunger and thirst, cold and heat, pleasure and pain.

Fasting

Some people engage in rigorous fasting practices. There is a special fast related to the moon. One starts with a full meal on a full moon day and gradually reduces the amount of food each day so that nothing is eaten on the new moon day. Then food is gradually increased again so that on the full moon day, a full meal is eaten. This is just one method of self-control. Some people try to live without eating food, but for those who want to practice yoga sincerely, a long period of fasting is not good. In God's creation, plants, animals, and humans naturally need food, so let us live our lives in a natural way. Fasting once a week or once in a fortnight is a good practice, and eating only fruits and fruit juices for a day is also beneficial.

A disciplined and dedicated life is the doorway to success. Disciplining the mind implies discipline of the body and discipline of *prana.* In the Bhagavad Gita (17:14–19), six types of penance or *tapah* are described in detail. *Tapah* is the process of disciplining the senses and the mind.

Physical or Bodily Discipline

In yogic practices, the body should be still and steady and not move without purpose. The restlessness of the body reflects the restlessness of the mind. Continuously moving your hands or feet while working or sitting on a chair are signs of a restless mind. Lord Buddha said, "If you cannot keep your hands and feet steady, how can you meditate?" During meditation, hands will often move knowingly or unknowingly. You may feel an itch somewhere and your hand will try to scratch it. It is not just the mind that becomes restless, but concentration is also impaired. When you sit and meditate, do not move your hands, even if you feel an itching sensation. It is well known that if you scratch one area of your body, you will soon feel itching somewhere else. You should practice keeping your body and your eyes under control, and not allow them to wander here and there without purpose. Swami Shriyukteshwarji said, "I have no time to blink my eyes." He used to sit with his eyes open for hours and hours in the state of *shambhavi.* How much control he must have had over his body, mind, and senses!

There are many who try to torture their bodies. Some will sit near fire in the heat of summer just to be able to develop tolerance to heat, while in winter they will sit in cold water, all to overcome the body's need for comfort.

There is a proverb in Sanskrit.

vishwamitra parasharah prabhritiyorvatambu-parnasanah
te´pi strímukhapankaja sulalitam drustva´pi mohamgata
salyannam saghruta dugdhadadhiyutayebhunjante manavah
tesam indriyanigraham yadi bhavet vindhyastare sagare

> "Great sages like Vishwamitra, Parashara, and others had so much self-control that they lived only on air and water. Despite this, they were still tempted at times to deviate from their path. If it is possible for ordinary people, who enjoy delicious food and drinks, sleep in comfortable beds, and enjoy a pleasant life to gain self-control and exercise self-discipline, then I would say that it is possible to move mountains and get them to float on the ocean."

The purpose of this proverb is to alert us to the power of the senses. We should exercise self-discipline by controlling our bodies, our eyes and our breath while always keeping our goal in mind. Just as impurities are removed from metal by heating it, the impurities of life are taken away by penance.

Simple Penance in Daily Life

Try to follow some rules of discipline, such as getting up early at a set time. Your body will protest and say, "Relax a little more," and your mind will remind you that it is the weekend. If you can just say "No!" and get up at the designated time anyway, this becomes a simple *tapah* in your daily life. Here in the ashram, meditation takes place early in the morning. Make a commitment that you will not come to meditation without first taking a shower. Follow you plan daily.

A long time ago, on *Guru Purnima Day*, I was in a Himalayan ashram. Approximately five hundred disciples were there and meditation started at 5:00 am.

Before beginning the class, the head of the monastery asked how many had taken a bath or shower before coming to the meditation class. About one hundred raised their hands. Then he asked how many of those had gone to river Ganga to take a bath. Ten people raised their hands. Then he said, "Let me make some observations. You all have come a great distance. Some of you have even come from another country, sacrificing some of your comforts to spend time in the holy company of monks and in the lap of the Himalayas on the banks of the Ganga. This is a rare opportunity, yet out of the five hundred people here, only ten people could avail themselves of the opportunity to bring some discipline into their lives."

Vangmaya Tapah, or the Discipline of Speech

In the Bhagavad Gita, Lord Krishna talks about the penance of speech and disciplining the mouth. Some people try to discipline the mouth during silent retreats, but this is only a partial discipline. During meals some people can be seen whispering. Keeping control over your tongue in both food and talk is not an easy task. Do not talk excessively and unnecessarily. Silent retreats provide you with a wonderful opportunity to remain silent.

Mental Tapah

Do not entertain negative thoughts, and do not speak about others in negative terms. Speak the truth, speak with love, and speak what is beneficial for others. Do not discuss the bad qualities of others in their absence.

The Inner Meaning of Tapah

The metaphorical meaning of *tapah* is to live in the *loka*, or the plane, of *tapah*. There are seven planes, or *lokas*, of existence which correspond to the seven chakras in the body. These are *bhuh loka* (the material plane), *bhuvah loka* (the plane above the material), *svah loka* (the plane of brilliance), *mahaḥ loka* (the plane of delusion), *janah loka* (the plane of ideas), *tapah loka* (the plane of meditation), and *satya loka* (the plane of experiencing truth). *Tapah loka* corresponds to the soul, or the *ajna chakra*. *Tapah* is also the practice of keeping the mind in the region between the soul center and the *sahasrara chakra*. This is the inner meaning of *tapah*.

The Benefits of Tapah

In Sadhana Pada (sutra 43), sage Patanjali speaks about the benefits of being established in *tapah*.

> *kayendriya siddhi ashuddhi kshaya tapasah*
>
> "As a result of *tapah*, special powers come to the body and the sense organs, and at the same time, any impurities found there, are removed."

Siddhi is the attainment of yogic or occult powers. It also means achieving perfection. Sage Patanjali described the threefold benefits of *tapah*, or the special skill of meditation, as follows:

1. *Kaya siddhi* — This is a special power of the body. By engaging in the practice of *tapah*, the abilities of the body increase in many ways.

The body becomes healthier and more beautiful, and physical activities are enhanced. A yogi can also make his body lighter or heavier at will, and it is said by many yogis that they can materialize and dematerialize their bodies at will.

Those who are acquainted with the life of Lahiri Mahasaya, a great householder yogi and master of Kriya Yoga, are no doubt aware of his physical abilities. Lahiri Mahasaya, while sitting in his office in India, could materialize in London. Babaji Maharaj could come into a room through locked doors. How were they able to do this? A story was told about an attorney who, while sleeping in his bedroom in Kolkata with a mosquito net fixed to his bed, felt something fall on him in the middle of the night. When he got up, he found a big stone on his bed that looked like it had been thrown there. He wondered where it had come from. Just then he saw a monk standing near him, who said, "I was going this way and I did it. Why are you so worried?" The attorney could not sleep because he kept thinking about it. Can the human mind comprehend how this could have happened? If I tell others, will they believe it? Who is he, and why did he come? What was the purpose of his actions? His ability is known as *kaya siddhi*, which comes after regular practice of meditation. However, you should not try to attain this, because it not the purpose of meditation. The ultimate goal cannot be to gain some sort of power, since power is only temporary.

2. *Indriya siddhi* is the attainment of perfection or the special power of the sense organs. God has given human beings five organs of perception and five organs of action. Although these sense organs are subtler than

the physical body, they are still limited in their functions by modern science and technology. Modern technology and science has provided us with telescopes to see farther, and telephones to hear voices that are far away. In this way, science and technology have increased the reach of sensory perception, just as yogis, with their yogic powers, wanted to increase the efficiency of the sense organs so they can see and hear subtler things. Normally, your eyes cannot see through a wall, but yogis who have *siddhis* can see and hear what is happening there. *Siddhis* can develop, but you should not try to make this happen. Even when *siddhis* come, the sincere yogi goes beyond them.

3. *Vasana kshaya* is the elimination of unnecessary desires. *Vasana* is 'desire' and *kshaya* is 'to destroy.' Human life is burgeoning with never-ending desires, unfulfilled wishes, ambitions, and expectations, which only make life miserable. An intelligent person should try to eliminate all unnecessary desires. There is a clear distinction between human need and human greed. Human needs are naturally limited, but human greed is without limit. A greedy human mind causes all sorts of problems, individually, socially, and globally. As long as our desires are not gradually cleansed and eliminated, we will not be able to attain peace and happiness, nor reach the goal of realization.

All human desires can be correlated with the different chakras or energy centers in the human spine and brain. There are five chakras in the spine and two chakras in the brain. The bottom chakra, known as *muladhara* or the money center, is where the desire for possession originates. In the second center, *svadhisthana chakra*, otherwise known as the family center, an endless desire for physical pleasure is to be found. The navel center, *manipura chakra,* is the source of the desire to taste various foods and intoxicating drinks, which also damage human health. The heart center, *anahata chakra*, is where emotional needs, the desire for friendship, and our likes and dislikes reside. The neck center, the *vishuddha chakra,* is the place of intellectual, religious, and philosophical pursuits, as well as a play of desire.

People whose minds are kept above the neck center will gradually be free from the temptations of their desires. By practicing *tapah*, you can gain control over your desires. If you have a strong sweet tooth and you refrain from eating sweets for some time, it is a way of gaining control over this desire. There is a tendency for someone who likes sweets to eat more of them when they are present, so try to do without for a period of time. If you like tea, try giving it up for awhile. It is the negation of desire. In the beginning your mind will react a little, but later it will cooperate. We can exercise self-control by practicing *tapah*, meditation, contemplation, and self-analysis. Desires are the cause of bondage, and by slowly eliminating them, liberation will be within your reach.

14

Svadhayaya: The Path of Self-Study

The Ninth Commandment

Knowledge is power. It has been observed that even plants have knowledge, since they adjust to seasonal changes. In autumn, they will drop their leaves to protect themselves from the cold of winter. When winter is over, new foliage will emerge, along with flowers and fruits. Animals have even more intelligence than plants, to say nothing of human beings! Knowledge, intellect, and the ability to discriminate between what is real and unreal, and what is right and wrong, can be of great benefit to human life. To gain such knowledge, one needs to keep the company of wise people and study books of wisdom. That is why sage Patanjali, while speaking about the beautification of human life, mentioned *svadhyaya*, or study, as an essential tool.

Svadhyaya is a word from the Vedas, which is used in the Bhagavad Gita, in Patanjali's Yoga Sutra, and in many other yogic books. In the Taittiriya Upanishad, this concept is used in a very beautiful way.

tapascha svadhyaya pravachane cha *(1:9:1)*
svadhyaya pravachana-bhyam na pramaditavyam *(1:11:1)*

> "Through your meditation, or *tapah,* continue *svadhyaya.* Never neglect *svadhyaya.*"

Svadhyaya has two meanings: *adhyaya* comes from *adhyayana,* which means 'to read' or 'to study.' So *svadhyaya* is 'to study oneself.' What should we study? People read so much and many have the habit of reading before sleeping. Merely reading a book is not *svadhyaya.* Because *svadhyaya* is defined as *moksha shastra adhyayana,* where *moksha* means 'liberation' and *shastra* means 'scripture,' the scriptures that help in giving us liberation should be studied.

Are there any scriptures that do not lead us to liberation? The answer is yes. In the Vedic tradition each human being has four objectives, namely, *dharma* (moral conduct), *artha* (material enjoyment), *kama* (the desire for pleasure), and *moksha* (liberation or freedom).

Our main purpose here is to gain our freedom. Scriptures that specifically deal with liberation, such as the Upanishads, the Bhagavad Gita, the Yoga Sutra, the Brahma Sutra, the Bhakti Sutra, the Quran, and the Bible, give us insights into how to live our lives and attain freedom.

How We Should Study

Both in ancient times and even today, just as we practice meditation with a qualified teacher, the scriptures were studied under the guidance of a teacher.

Scriptures often have layers of meaning and to gain an understanding beyond the surface meaning is not easy. When Jesus was asked by his disciples why he spoke in parables, he replied that they are not for everyone. (Mark 4:10–12). He told them, "The secret of the Kingdom of God has been given to you. But to those on the outside everything is said in parables so that, 'they may be ever seeing but never perceiving, and ever hearing but never understanding.'" In another place (John 6:56), Jesus said, "Whoever eats my flesh and drinks my blood remains in me, and I in him." If one takes Jesus' statements literally, they cannot be understood. Many people left Jesus because of this teaching, leaving only a very few who understood. Then Jesus asked them, "You do not want to leave, do you?" (John 6:67) "Simon Peter answered him, "Lord, to whom shall we go? You have the words of eternal life. We believe and know that you are the Holy One of God." (John 6:68–69) Anyone can purchase a book and read it, but how many can truly understand what is inside?

Japa or Chanting

One meaning of *svadhyaya* is to study the scriptures that bring you freedom under the guidance of a teacher. Another meaning is to do *japa* or recite the name of God. In the Yoga Sutra of Patanjali, Samadhi Pada (sutra 28), it states:

> *tat japah tat artha bhavanam*
>
> "Chant that (mantra, *om*) with contemplation on its meaning."

Many people chant, and chanting with the rosary is a common practice in almost all religions. Sage Patanjali said to chant with contemplation on the meaning of the mantra. Saint Kabir said:

mala to hath me phire jibh phire mukh mahi
manua to chau dishi phire ye to sumiran nahi

"The mind roams in all four directions, which are not visible to the person."

Chanting can be of three types. Firstly, there is audible chanting, which can be heard by others. Secondly, there is silent chanting, where just the lips and tongue move, but no sound is made. Finally, there is mental chanting, which is neither audible nor outwardly visible, where scripture or a mantra is heard in the mind. It is almost like meditation. Whether it is the chanting of scriptures or the chanting of a mantra, one can use all three methods.

Svadhyaya as Self-Study

Sva means 'self' and *adhyaya* is 'to study.' What does it mean? The world is the university and your life is the book. You have to study the book of your life in the university of this world to acquire knowledge of yourself. Paramahamsa Hariharananda often quoted a stanza from Alexander Pope's song, *Psalms of Life*:

"Know thyself. Presume not God to scan.
The proper study of mankind is man"

So, embark on a course of self-study. How do you study yourself? What does it mean? Observe your breath, your mind, your thoughts, your behavior, and your speech. Try to understand what is going on, and realize who you are. This is real *svadhyaya.*

The Benefits of Svadhyaya

In the Yoga Sutra of Patanjali, the results of engaging in the practice of *svadhyaya*, or trying to know oneself in every breath, are found. So, what will happen? Sutra 44 in Sadhana Pada says:

svadhyayat ishta samprayogah

"As a result of self-study, one will receive a vision of the Divine in the form of one's chosen deity."

You will receive the vision of the deity you love. If you love Jesus, or Mother Mary, as your own personal deity, this is who you will see. If you love Lord Rama, Lord Krishna, or Lord Buddha as your own, you will have a vision of them. But this is not enough, since any vision you have will come and go, and that which has a beginning always has an end. The Bhagavad Gita states: To have a vision might give you joy but it is not permanent. You may have had a nice dream, and when you got up, you were very happy, but how long will this last?

Ishta samprayoga: 'having a vision of the chosen deity' is the ordinary meaning, but *samprayoga* also has another meaning: *prayoga* means 'to apply' and *samprayoga* means 'thorough application.' If you study the scriptures and study yourself daily, what will happen? You will learn to apply yourself in a divine way in your thought, words, and deeds. Every thought will be divine, and you will see everything as a personification of divinity. More love will manifest. Distance and difference will decrease. I see my beloved, my reflection in everything I look upon. This will develop by self-study and studying the scriptures, which is accompanied by meditation. Make a habit of studying the scriptures at least for a short time each day. When I was a little boy, my mother would quote a proverb in Oriya: "Whether you like it or not, eat something bitter every day." When the opportunity comes to study with a teacher, be happy. Otherwise, study alone, and trust that God will help you.

Once Shri Chaitanya, a great incarnation of God who was traveling through South India, went into a temple and saw a person holding the scriptures upside down, with tears rolling down his cheeks. Shri Chaitanya became curious. What was he doing? Surely he was not reading, yet tears were rolling down his face and he was experiencing something. Shri Chaitanya waited until the man regained his normal composure, and asked, "My brother, what were you studying?"

The man replied, "The Bhagavad Gita."

"Did you really study it? You were holding the book upside down," said Shri Chaitanya

"What is there to study? I was seeing the Gita," said the man.

"What did you see?" asked Shri Chaitanya.

"I saw the complete battlefield, and Lord Krishna was standing near Arjuna."

Just by holding the book, even upside down, he was able to see and hear. This is only possible through love. Any practice done without love will not yield enough love. Always practice with love. Love is the most important principle of spiritual life. Study the scriptures and understand their meaning, not as you would a storybook or novel, but by penetrating to the deeper layers of their wisdom. Read a little at a time and then contemplate it. Try to apply the knowledge you have gained in your daily life. Suppose you read Jesus' statement, "Love your enemies," in the Bible. (Matthew 5:44) This one sentence is enough, and it is not difficult to understand it. Think about it. Who is your enemy? Where is your enemy? How will you love your enemy? Put this into practice in daily life, and you will soon experience divinity everywhere.

Knowledge is the seed which grows into the tree of realization. Knowledge should be put into practice. If it is not put into practice, knowledge just becomes theory. With sincere practice, one will become humble and be ready for an experience of the Divine.

15

Ishwara Pranidhana: The Path of Surrender to the Divine

The Tenth Commandment

On the spiritual path, love or devotion is considered to be a very effective method for obtaining realization. On the path of devotion, God is seen as the Supreme Being, and every breath is spent channeling one's devotion toward one's Beloved, God. That is why it is said in the Bible (Luke 10:27), "Love the Lord your God with all your heart..." In the Yoga Sutra, sage Patanjali is speaking of *ishwara pranidhana,* or surrender to God, as the last *niyama* or moral principle.

Before explaining the practice of *ishwara pranidhana,* I will tell about a song that Ramakrishna Paramahamsa loved. This song emphasizes that devotion, or pure love for God, is even rarer than attaining liberation. In his song God says: "I can give you liberation very easily, but I hesitate to give you pure love." Let your heart and mind be full of love, let your thoughts be full of love, and let your activities be full of love. Love is God and God is love.

Love is sweeter than any sweetmeat. In India, people eat many types of sweets with their meals. In the Ayurvedic practice of eating, the first dish that is served is bitter food, followed by green vegetables, and then by protein and carbohydrates simultaneously. This is then followed by eating yogurt or something sour, and finally by dessert. *Madhurena samaptayet:* "Finish your meal with a little sweet." In India, therefore, a meal is not complete without a sweet.

This can also be applied as a metaphor to daily life. People begin their lives with love, and it should continue right to the end with love. Yoga is a philosophy, a psychology, a discipline, and a way of life. Yoga is not just a set of exercises, but helps us to live our lives in the right manner.

The tenth commandment, *íshwara pranidhana,* is difficult to translate. *Ishwara* is usually translated as 'God,' but in Vedic culture, God the Absolute or Brahman, is completely neutral. When Brahman manifests as activity or creation, that aspect is known as *ishwara. Ishwara* is the one who controls and regulates everything. In English we would say God, but there is a distinction to be made here, so we could translate it as the 'Lord,' or 'God the Lord.' The root word *pranidhana* has multiple meanings, namely, 'to bow down,' 'to apply,' 'to surrender,' 'to offer,' and 'to be humble,' and refers to the process of bowing, making offerings, applying oneself, surrendering, and also loving. Taken together, *ishwara pranidhana* means applying oneself for God, and surrendering and offering everything to God.

The following three examples teach us how to keep our mind on God while working.

In a village I have seen how a cow and her newborn calf interact. The calf will move around and the cow may be eating, but if you go anywhere near the calf, the cow will immediately give you a warning look. She remains aware of the calf even while she is eating.

There is another example that Ramakrishna Paramahamsa often repeated. A maidservant had a child of her own, but had to leave her child to take care of her master's child. Although she was physically attending to the child of the master, mentally she was absorbed in the thoughts of her own son.

A young mother may be cooking, but her attention is always on her baby sleeping in the next room, and if the baby makes the slightest sound, the mother will leave her cooking and run to the room to attend to her baby.

In every breath, and in every moment, we should be conscious of Who am I? Where am I? Those who are steadfast in this enquiry, and yearn to find the answer, will succeed.

People feel so much pain when they are separated from their friends, yet the separation from God that we experience is a separation out of ignorance, since God is actually eternally present in all and all around us. A song that Tagore used to sing illustrates this point:

> *"You were hiding in my heart and I did not look for you;*
> *I looked outside and forgot you.*
> *You were always present with me, in my pleasure and pain,*
> *but looking outside I felt pain over such little things.*
> *Now I realize my mistake, you are mine and I am Thine."*

How is it possible to surrender and apply divinity in every step of life? If ego is present, it is not possible. This is shown in the following story from the Ramayana, when Lord Rama, his wife Sita, and brother Lakshmana were in exile and walking in the forest. Lakshmana was not able to see Lord Rama because Sita was in between. In this example, Lord Rama is God, while Sita represents God's illusive power, and Lakshmana is the individual. So when we are looking at Sita, we cannot see Lord Rama. When we are ruled by our ego or ignorance, we cannot see God. The ego is concerned with 'me and mine.' It is alright to use the word 'my,' but the feeling of attachment which usually accompanies the word 'my' comes from ego and increases ignorance, which does not help us to surrender to God.

Those who offer every breath and everything they have, whether good or bad, to God, thinking, "Nothing belongs to me, my body is Your gift to me, my breath is

Your blessing, this look is Your look, and when tears stream down my face, they are Your tears; nothing belongs to me"; they are the ones who have really surrendered and become free of their egos.

Although this is considered to be the tenth step, this feeling of surrender should accompany all the previous steps. Sleep with God, get up with God, dream of God, and move with God. In the Old Testament it is often said that both Jacob and Noah walked with God. How can you walk with God if God is not a person? Walking with God entails constantly being in God consciousness, and not losing this connection even when involved in worldly affairs. In reality, the wave and the ocean are inseparable. Whenever you think you are the wave, you have separated yourself from the ocean.

This teaching of *ishwara pranidhana*, or surrender to God, is a wonderful practice and is repeatedly mentioned in the Yoga Sutra. When he described Kriya Yoga, sage Patanjali said, *tapah svadhyaya ishwara pranidhanani kriya yogah* (Sadhana Pada Sutra 1), and when he spoke of the attainment of *samadhi*, he also said *ishwara pranidhanat va* (Samadhi Pada Sutra 23), which means that only with complete surrender to God can one attain *samadhi*. Therefore, every sincere seeker should remember this message and cultivate love for God.

The Benefits of Ishwara Pranidhana

What will happen if you put this into practice? According to the Sadhana Pada (sutra 45):

> *samadhi siddhih ishwara pranidhana*
>
> "When you have completely surrendered to God, you will achieve the state of *samadhi* or realization."

You will attain perfection. *Ishwara pranidhana* means to remember God in every breath, to love God in sleep, in wakeful and dream states and even in the deep sleep state. Without love, perfection is impossible. Through love and surrender and eliminating ego, you can achieve this. *Ishwara pranidhana* is not just a topic for discussion. We have discussed it now as a philosophy in order to understand it, but it has to be applied in life. By only listening and reading, we will get to know the theory, but if it is not put into practice, it will be of no use to us.

There is a beautiful song written in Bengali that my master Baba Hariharanandaji was fond of.

In the Flow of Divine Love

premdhan bilay gora ray
chand nitayi dake aye aye
premdhan bilay gora ray.

prem ke nebire aye,
dekheja dekheja premer nadi boye jaye
prem koloshe, koloshe dhale tobu na phuraye re.
se je gour premer ban,
bhasiye diye ayere tora jato yi abhiman
preme shantipur dubu dubu nade bhese jaye re
(oi) shantipur dubu, dubu nade bhese jaye re.

sab bhasiye ayere tora, bhenge diye mayar kara
prem sagare keo marena mare benche jaye re

In the Flow of Divine Love (Translation)

Gora Ray spreads the treasure of love,
Nitai Chand is calling all, "Come, come..."

Come, whoever wants love. Come, and see how the river of love flowing.
He pours the nectar of love from vessel to vessel,
Yet love is endless.

That is the wave of love of Gouranga.
Let all your ego and pride drift away in this current of love.
(This) Shantipur is drowned in the flood of love,
The village Nadia is over flooded by this river of divine love.

Let all of yours (attachments) flow down.
Break the shackles of the prison of *maya.*
No one dies in the ocean of love, but survives.

According to the song, Shri Chaitanya is distributing love. Anyone who is interested can come and get it. He is pouring the nectar of love from a pitcher that is always full and never runs out. His presence brings an overflow of love. This flow of love resides in the heart of every seeker. If you can find that source of love and devotion within, it will become an unending source of joy and bliss. The more you love, the more intense this love will become. The more you love others, the more you will want to give love to all. Give up your ego and your pride, and jump into those waters in which no one dies. It is only your negative qualities which die. Let your thoughts be full of love, let your words be full of love, let your deeds be full of love, and let your life be full of love.

16

Be a Yogi

The Bhagavad Gita is a complete, sacred scripture for humanity as a whole. It contains the highest form of knowledge and provides guidance for people from all walks of life, especially spiritual seekers. Lord Krishna is the preceptor, the eternal guide, and Arjuna is the seeker of truth. In the form of conversations, discussions, and questions and answers, the truth of life is examined. There are many times when Lord Krishna directs Arjuna to act in a perfect way. At one point Lord Krishna says:

> *tapasvibhyodhiko yogi jnanibhyopi matodhikah*
> *karmibhyaschadhika yogi tasmad yogi bhavarjuna*
> *(6:46)*

> "A yogi is greater than the *tapasvi*, those who perform austerities and penance, greater even than the *jnani*, the knower of truth. He is also superior to the *karmi*, who celebrates *yajna* and other rituals. O Arjuna! Be thou a yogi."

This may raise questions in a seeker as to what exactly yoga is, and how and why one should put it into practice.

Yoga is a practical science. The ordinary meaning of yoga is 'union' or 'addition.' The simple meaning is *jiva atmani eva aikyam:* the union of *jiva* with *atman*, the individual consciousness with the Supreme consciousness, *ham* with *sa*, the body with the soul, is yoga. In the scriptures it is said that there are 108 yogas. The direct guidance of a realized and perfect master is necessary for the practice of yoga. All of the 108 yogas sometimes cannot be practiced since there is no longer a perfect master in that line. Furthermore, it would not be possible to follow all yogas, due to the many difficulties encountered during our short human lives. The scriptures declare that *yat sarvabhutam tad grahitabyam:* that the essence of the teachings must be accepted and put into practice.

What is the essence of all yogas? The scientific technique of Kriya Yoga has both theoretical and practical aspects that can only be learned and practiced with the able guidance of a realized and experienced master. The philosophy of Kriya Yoga is very simple to follow. Human beings perform actions ceaselessly from birth until death. Neither the body nor the soul can function alone. Neither the bulb nor electricity alone, could give us light. Just as the union of the bulb and the electricity gives us light, so the body and soul joined in the state of *yogastha*, perform every action. So the real 'doer' is the soul, and the body is the instrument.

This is a practical technique. In all our actions, we should perceive the soul, but due to ignorance, the *jiva* thinks it is the one who performs all actions. This is nothing but ego, *aham karta iti bhavah,* and this binds the *jiva,* so it must take birth again and again in order to reap what it has sown, and experience the results of past actions. However, if the soul is perceived in all actions, then the soul, and not the *jiva,* enjoys the fruit of past actions.

The technique of Kriya Yoga is self-liberating and bestows peace, joy, and bliss upon us. Those who practice Kriya Yoga will experience the simultaneous development of body, mind, and intellect and have awareness of the soul. They will be free from the chain of cause and effect, and will experience constant liberation and Self-realization. So Lord Krishna commands his perfect disciple, Arjuna, to be a yogi: *tasmad yogi bhavarjuna,* O Arjuna! Be a yogi.

17

How to Lead a God-Conscious and Moral Lifestyle

With deep love, remember God and the masters. We all are children of God, and we all are beautiful. Although we all have come into this world, it is not our permanent home, and one day, we will have to leave. We all have come here to play our different roles in life. Let us pray to God to give us balance and harmony in our lives, and to live our lives in a loving way.

The life of Paramahamsa Hariharananda is a message in itself. His was a life of perfection, a life of constant God consciousness, and an example of putting the principles of Kriya Yoga into practice. He lived among us and taught us how to live always with the consciousness of God. Spiritual life is not a figment of the imagination. It is not a dream. It is reality, and to be in this reality, you should live with constant awareness of the presence of God.

Before we came into this world, when we all were in our mothers' wombs, we all were yogis. During this time we spent months in prayer and meditation, but many of us may not be aware of that. Because of that period of prayer and meditation prior to birth, a baby is so peaceful and loving when it comes into this world. Once we come into this world again, we forget to remember God, to love God, and to live a God-conscious life. Life itself is beautiful, but who really understands it? We live with ego, emotion, and ignorance, which simultaneously cloud our consciousness, and cause us a lot of suffering.

How can we transform our lives? How can we live a better life? We should be conscious of our own divinity and be aware of the nature of the world, and live our lives accordingly. My master, Gurudev Paramahamsa Hariharananda, once told me, "I grew up in a good family. I had wonderful parents and my brothers and sisters were unimaginably beautiful. We had so much love for each other, but I left them." I asked him why he left, despite being surrounded by so many good people and so much love. He answered, "Have you heard about business? When it is a company, they call it a "public limited" or "private limited" company. So my company in the beginning was limited, but now it is unlimited.

Small things will not bring lasting satisfaction. A small trifle of a thing is just not enough to give you the experience of real joy. Real joy only comes from beholding the Absolute. People tend to settle for little things to make them happy, but then quickly grow disappointed. People often think a new job will bring them happiness, but when they realize the job is not that good, they are no longer happy.

Gurudev then added, "I left everything, but I also gained everything. I left one mother, and I got so many more mothers. I left one family, and I became a part of an even larger family. I left behind a few siblings, and I got so many more brothers and sisters. If you cannot leave everything, you will not be able to experience the truth and be free."

Why did he leave? Surely he left for some higher purpose. Try to cultivate the attitude that you should not hold on to things. Learn how to live. If you never exhaled, you would not be able to inhale. If the food you ate were not digested and excreted, you would not be able to eat. There simply would be no room for fresh air or food. So, spiritual life is an inner journey and a life of detachment made for a higher purpose. This journey is not confined to just one hour of practice every day, but should be continuous. Spiritual life is a never ending journey.

What happens in spiritual life? One night two young men set off in a boat with the desire to visit some different places. Throughout the night, while on their journey, they consumed some intoxicating substances to enhance their enjoyment. Slowly the darkness faded and turned to light. When they looked around, one friend said to the other, "Do you know this new place looks so much like our village. The trees, the surroundings, and the landscape all look similar." What!" declared the other, "that can't be." They both sat up, and as they looked around, they realized what they had done. They had been rowing the entire night, but had forgotten to untie the anchor. Spiritual life is like that. If you want to embark on the journey, you have to untie your anchor, and leave the old, familiar things behind you.

What is the significance of untying the anchor? When we start our journey and visit new people and places, we tend to take with us a souvenir which reminds us of that place, and carry it in our luggage. When we visit the next place, we acquire another souvenir and carry it with us. The same process goes on in our minds.

When you attend a spiritual program or retreat, you will carry some memory of it in your mind. Anything that happens in our lives is stored in our memory. Our memories can cause us many problems. We should be intelligent about our memories and arrange them like books on a shelf. The books you want to use or read are kept close at hand, while the others which are not needed are kept elsewhere or even given to someone else. The big problem with our memory is that we remember what we should forget, and forget what we should remember. What should we remember, and what should we forget? We should forget and eliminate all of our negative qualities, such as anger, selfishness, jealously, greed, and unhappiness. Suppose you have some dirt on your hands and you want to clean it off. To do this, you will need some soap and water. You can wash your hands, and they will soon be clean. Similarly, to live a moral life is to be good, to see good, and to do good.

There was a monk in India whose simple teaching was: be good and do good. When monks of his ashram presented his books to the President of India, he said, "It is written 'Be good. Do good.' If one only does good, is that not enough? Why is it necessary to also be good?" The monks replied, "If one is not good, one cannot do good. If the food is not of good quality, it will not taste good, nor will it be good for you. So, firstly, it should be good. Be good, and then, do good." And this is exactly the point that we miss in our lives.

Let us try to understand this a little bit better. Be good. Do good. See good. This is the way to God. What is the meaning of being good? Sometimes when I ask people, "How are you?" they reply, "Not good." "What has happened?" I ask. "One of my family members died," or "My health is not good," or "I got a letter from my employer. I have only two weeks left on my job."

Now, let us think, is this the first time that a family member has died? Has not your grandfather and great-grandfather died?

I will tell you about the death of my father. When I went to see him in hospital, he said, "I was waiting for you. I am so happy that you have come. I have seen you, and I am happy. I am going." I was willing to sit a little longer with him. He simply said, "You can go. I am going, so why sit here longer with me? If you can be with others, you can do something good for them." He died the next day. Was I unhappy?

Death is not a new thing. Disease is not a new thing. Wrinkles on your face are not a new thing either, and neither is losing your job. So why are we so sad about these things? It is because we do not understand what 'good' really is. Real good is remaining in the presence of God within. There is really no difference between God and good. In English, they say God is good. If God is good, then when you say "good morning," you are beginning the morning with God. How can you begin the day in this way? Start your morning with prayer. Spiritual life is a life of constant thanksgiving. In every breath thank God.

I will tell you a story about a minister. Long ago there was a king who had a very wise, God-loving minister. No matter what happened to him, he always thanked God. If he had a fever, he used to say, "Thank God that I have a fever today, because I was so proud of my health before. Now I have remembered that good health is not permanent." One day the king and the minister went hunting. The king tried to shoot an arrow and, because he was not mindful, he injured his finger and it started to bleed. The king complained about how much his finger hurt. "Thank God that you have a wound in your hand," said the minister. The king was so upset with the minister for thanking God for his pain, that he tied the minister's hands and feet and left him in the forest. When the king was going through the forest alone, he met some tribal people. A king only has power when he is surrounded by his people, but being alone, they captured him, and tied him up with a rope to use as a sacrifice. The king was thinking, "O God! What am I going to do?" The tribal priest came and inspected the king, but when he noticed the wound and the blood on his finger, he decreed that the king was unfit to sacrifice. So they untied the king and set him free. The king kept saying, "Thank God that I have wounded my finger; otherwise I would have lost my life there." He remembered his minister and went to look for him. The king found him, and after he untied him, he apologized and told him the story of what had happened. Then the minister said, "Thank God that you tied me up and left me in the forest. If you had not tied me up, they would have left you and they would have sacrificed me instead." Often, we do not understand our lives and ask ourselves, "Why is this happening to me?" A spiritual person accepts what is happening and lives a life of constant thanksgiving.

Gurudev used to say, "O God, even if my hands are full with many things, let me not succumb to ego. Let me remember you always."

Let us think a little. Why do we have an ego? People have an ego about their beauty. Yes, you may be beautiful at the moment, but since you know that it is not permanent, why have an ego about your beauty? Why not thank God for this gift of beauty? You may have an ego about being young and not having a care in the world, but this too will pass and be lost one day.

A young man strutting along with a lot of pride saw an old woman who was walking hunched over, as if she were searching for something. The young man asked the woman, "What are you searching for? Can I help you?" But his voice betrayed his pride and vanity. The old woman looked at him and said, "I have lost my treasure." "What kind of treasure? Where did you lose it?" asked the man. She said, "My foolish child, I have lost my youth and my strength."

You may have a lot of money, but why have an ego about it? Why not be nice to people and do something good with what you have?

Gurudev often said, "My hands might be filled with many things, but let me not have an ego. Bless me, O God, that I should not forget you. Let me think of you in the wakeful state; let me not forget you, even in my dreams." This was Gurudev's prayer, to live a God-conscious life day and night, from breath to breath. This is also the message of Kriya Yoga, and the point of spiritual life — to be good, so that goodness will manifest more by doing good.

God has given us a good mind with which to think. What do you think about? God has given us eyes to see. What do you see when you look around? God has given us a mouth to speak. What sort of things do you say? God has given us ears with which to hear. What do you hear? God has given us hands to work. What do you do? God has given so many capabilities and talents. Use everything that has been given to you to see and hear good, to think and say good things, and to do good. This is what spiritual life is all about. It is in your hands.

Often, people will complain that thoughts arise and disturb them when they sit for meditation, and they want to know how to get rid of these thoughts. A spiritual master was asked the same question. The spiritual master offered a simple solution. Since these worldly thoughts about family, work, and other matters come during meditation time, just reverse the process, so that when you are at work, or talking to friends, or cooking, eating, and doing other things, simply think of God. If you can think of God while engaging in worldly activities, then during your meditation, worldly thoughts will not come to you. With practice, this process of reversal will work. Gurudev said, "Practice, practice, practice. Practice brings perfection. Through practice, you will behold the divine goal." He also said, "An ounce of practice is better than tons of theories." Gurudev has repeatedly told us to watch our breath. Have you been conscious of your breath while you were reading this? If we are not conscious of divinity, everything is really pointless.

Gurudev's message is to love God continuously through your breath. If there is no breath in your body, you have nothing. Gurudev said that breath is your beauty. If there is no breath, your beauty will be gone. Your body will die if there is no breath. Your breath is your strength, since it enables you to work. Your breath is also your brainpower, so love your breath. Our breath goes in and out day and night, but we are not aware of the value of our breath. If there is anything of real value to you, it is not your memory, or intelligence. It is not your possessions or bank balance. It is not your family or friends. It is your breath. If there is no breath, you will have nothing. Our breath is so valuable, yet we ignore it constantly. Love your breath — it is not really that difficult. Nobody is telling you to keep your head down and legs up, or to fast, in order to be spiritual. To be spiritual is to be aware of spirit. Spirit means breath. Let us try to practice with every breath the awareness that we are divine. If I am conscious that I am divine, how can anger and ego arise? Remember, it is when you forget that all your troubles begin. When we are aware of our problems, we can deal with them. Let us be aware of our inner divinity and our role in this world. Let us be aware that this journey of ours is temporary.

Pray, "O my beloved teacher! Show me the path of love and the path of spirituality." In this world there are many roads on which to travel. People will always tell you that their way is the best way, and so we become confused. Ask, "Tell me, my teacher, what is really good? What should we do?" We have to follow the master's instructions and face all of our negative qualities with strength and honesty. We have to overcome our negative qualities and become conscious of our divinity. We have come to this world, and in the process, we have forgotten our connection to God. We have to live in this world with constant awareness. Time passes so quickly, so do not waste time. Breathe every breath with love. This is the teaching of the masters. Waste time with none but God, then time will not be wasted. Let us try to practice this constantly.

18

Epilogue

We have discussed the ten practices or the ten commandments of yoga; five of them as an aspect of *yama* and *niyama*, which are the first two fundamental limbs of the eightfold path of Ashtanga Yoga. We have also examined the benefits that come from following and being firmly established in these ten practices described in the Yoga Sutra of Patanjali. To recapitulate, the Ten Commandments as described by sage Patanjali are:

1. *Ahimsa* — non-injury or nonviolence in thought, word, and deed. The benefit coming from this practice is that in the presence of such a person, enmity cannot exist.

2. *Satyam* or truthfulness — the benefit of this practice is purity of speech and that what one says will come true.

3. *Asteya* or not stealing — not to be greedy or covet others' possessions or property. The benefit this

brings is that prosperity is gained without excessive effort.

4. *Brahmacharya* or celibacy or continence — the benefit of this practice is strength and vitality.

5. *Aparigraha* or not accepting gifts and having no expectations — the benefit of this practice is to give knowledge of the past and future.

6. *Shaucham* or external and internal purity — the benefit is cultivating inner detachment towards one's own body and about close contact with others.

7. *Santosha* or contentment — the benefit this brings is happiness beyond comparison.

8. *Tapah* or self-mortification and penance — the benefit of this practice is the removal of impurities and an increase in the power of concentration and calmness.

9. *Svadhyaya* or self-study and the study of scriptures which reveal the path of liberation — the benefit this brings is having a vision of your chosen deity.

10. *Ishwara Pranidhana* or surrender to God — the benefit this brings is *samadhi* or the state of bliss.

Who can achieve these ten commandments? Is it possible? Is it too late? Are we too old? A classical book on yoga written by Svatmarama Yogendra known as Hatha Yoga Pradipika says:

yuva vruddhotivruddhah va vyadhitah durbalopi va
abhyasat siddhim apnoti sarva yogeshu atandritah
(1:64)

"Whether one is young or old, extremely weak or sick, if one is practicing sincerely and regularly, avoiding sloth and laziness, one will surely achieve success; there is no doubt about it."

Verse 65 again reassures that it is not impossible:

kriya yuktasya siddhih — One who is practicing kriya gets success.

syat akriyasya katham bhavet — Without practice how can it be?

na shastra patha matrena — Only by discussing the scripture,

yoga siddhih prajayate — One cannot attain success.

In this context, "kriya" means the kriya technique, and kriya also means practice. You know many things, but you don't practice. If you are suffering from a disease and you leave the medicine in your pocket without taking it, will you be cured? A successful doctor is one who knows how to use his knowledge. If one does not apply knowledge, it is of less use.

Lahiri Mahasaya said, *hardam laga rahore bhai banat banat banjayi:* "Practice yoga in every breath. Through this practice you will achieve perfection."

Where is your mind? Are you conscious of your breath? If you apply all the discipline that we discussed and change your habits, success is inevitable. In every step you will get success, joy, happiness, and contentment. Every moment is a state of joy. You will attain *anupama sukhatvam* (superlative happiness) if you practice daily, regularly, and sincerely.

My master, Baba Hariharananda, used to often say that human life is short, difficulties are many, and one should not waste precious human life with unnecessary worries, emotions, fears, and frustrations. One should be disciplined. One should be committed to achieve the goal of life. Success and failure are in one's own hand. A weak person fails in every step and a strong and courageous person, in spite of difficulties and troubles, with sincere effort succeeds in life. We are not only human beings, we are children of God. We have God-like potentialities. We are loving and divine. We should realize this and manifest the divine qualities through the practice of sincere prayer and meditation. No matter what conditions in life that we may be facing, we can achieve our goal with strong determination and dedicated effort.

sarve bhavantu sukhinah sarve santu niramayah
sarve bhadrani pashyantu ma kashchid duhkha bhag bhavet

> "May all be happy, may all be healthy, may all see only auspicious sights, and may no one have a share in sorrow."

Glossary

Ahimsa	non (a-) violence (*himsa*), non-injury to others in thought, word, or deed
Alasya	dullness; lacking vitality and strength; one of the obstacles of yoga
Anahata chakra	("wheel of the unstruck [sound]"): the dorsal (heart) center
Anupamasukhatvam	superlative happiness
Aparigraha	the principle of not accepting gifts from others
Artha	material prosperity; to earn wealth in a righteous way; one of the four vital accomplishments in human life
Asana	("seat") sitting; posture; a place to sit for prayer and

	meditation; the third limb of Patanjali's Ashtanga Yoga system
Ashrama	a stage of human life
Asteya	the principle of not stealing and not coveting another's property
Ashtanga Yoga	("eight limbs of yoga"): eightfold disciplines or aspects of the path of complete spiritual development propounded by sage Patanjali, i.e., *yama, niyama, asana, pranayama, pratyahara, dharana, dhyana,* and *samadhi*
Atma; atman	("Self"): the soul; indwelling spirit
Ayurveda	("life science"): medicine of mind, body, and soul; one of the *upavedas*, divinely revealed sciences in India
Bandha	contracting or expanding a part of the body purposefully through the breath
Bhakti	devotion; a path of experiencing pure divine love for God

Bhuh loka	the first of the seven upper spheres of existence (*loka*); corresponds to the money (earth) center; material plane
Bhuvah loka	the second of the seven upper spheres of existence (*loka*); corresponds to the procreation (water) center
Brahmachari	one who observes the vow of *brahmacharya*
Brahmacharya	abstinence or perpetual celibacy, sense control; *brahmacharya* means "to roam (*char*) in God (*Brahma*)," metaphorically to live in constant God consciousness
Brahmacharya ashrama	the life of studenthood with strict discipline
Brahman	God, the Ultimate Absolute, the formless Spirit; derived from the root *brih*, "to grow" or "to expand"
Brahmin	the first caste in the ancient Vedic social system of priests and teachers; metaphorically those who are on the spiritual path; to be established in God (*Brahman*)

Chaturanga Yoga	("four limbs"): refers to the last four limbs of the Ashtanga Yoga system
Dharana	concentration; the sixth limb of Patanjali's Ashtanga Yoga system
Dharma	ordinarily translated as religion, righteousness, discipline; divine law; *dharma* comes from *dhri*, which means the power of receptivity, and *man*, which means life. Thus *dharma* means "that which upholds", i.e. the breath. Breath is the true religion.
Dhyana	meditation; contemplation; the seventh limb of Patanjali's Ashtanga Yoga system
Ekanga Yoga	one-limbed yoga; easiest form of yoga which is based on the primordial sound *om*
Grihastha ashrama	the life of householder with self-sacrifice
Guru Purnima	full moon day in the month of July, birthday of sage Vyasa
Ham	the gross body or instrument of the soul. The soul is the doer and the gross body is the instrument. *Ham* also refers to

	the ego, the false identification of the soul with the gross body.
Hamsa	the material perishable body is *ham.* The power by which you inhale through your nose is *sa*, which refers to the soul. In the *hamsa* stage you forget your existence and feel that *sa*, inhalation, is the life of the gross body.
Himsa	("harm") maliciousness, injury
Indriya siddhi	attainment of perfection or special power of the sense organs to perceive subtler things
Ishwara	("foremost ruler"): the ruler of the universe
Ishwara pranidhana	surrender to God or cultivating the path of devotion
Janah loka	the fifth of the seven upper spheres of existence (*loka*); corresponds to the neck (ether) center; plane of ideas
Japa	("recitation"): chanting and remembering the holy name of God, as in a mantra
Jiva	the individual soul

Jnana	first step of *prajna* (wisdom); acquisition of spiritual knowledge
Jnani	the knower of truth
Jyoti mudra	the process of regulating, controlling, and channeling the energy of the nine doors
Kaivalya	("aloneness"): the highest state of God consciousness; the Supreme
Kala	principle of time, death, the lord of death
Kama	desire for pleasure
Karma	action; duty; the law of cause and effect
Karmi	one who celebrates *yajnas* and rituals
Kaya siddhi	special powers of the body
Khechari mudra	special *mudra* practiced in yoga. The tongue is pointed towards the fontanel. It is derived from *kha* ("space") and *char* ("to roam") — to roam in the inner space, vacuum of meditation.
Kriya Yoga	the science of self-control and Self-realization through meditation

Loka	a plane of existence corresponding to one of the seven chakras in the body
Mahabhasya	a commentary on the Ashtadhyayi, a book of Sanskrit grammar written by a linguist and grammarian named Panini
Maha mudra	("great seal"): the yogic technique of physical, astral, and causal purification
Mahah loka	the fourth of the seven upper spheres of existence (*loka*); corresponds to the emotion (air) center; plane of delusion
Manipura chakra	("wheel of the jeweled city"): the lumbar (stomach) center
Moha	delusion, dejection, and infatuation
Moksha	liberation; the state of complete soul awareness, emancipation, and *samadhi*; freedom from the bondage and attachment that arise from delusion
Mudra ("seal")	position of body and hands
Muladhara chakra	("wheel of the root (*mula*) foundation (*dhara*)") the coccygeal (money) center

Naisthika brahmacharya	strict *brahmacharya* or abstinence, living more in meditation, prayer, and God consciousness
Niyama	("restraint"): principles of self-restraint; the second limb of Patanjali's Ashtanga Yoga system, which includes purity, contentment, austerity, self-study, and surrender to God
Om	also written *AUM* — this represents the three bodies of every human being or the triple divine qualities. *A* is the causal body (sound), *U* is the astral body (vibration), and *M* is the physical body (light).
Pada	the feet; pillars; the world
Prakriti	("creative force"): the veil of nature, or the material substratum of creation, consisting of the three *gunas*
Pramada	confusion or doubt
Prana	("life"): the life-force, vital breath, vital air; one of the five main *pranas* (vital energies), responsible for absorption; metaphorically, *prana* refers to exhalation

Pranava	*Om*
Pranayama	("restraint of *prana*"): regulation of breath through control of the life force (*prana*); the fourth limb of Patanjali's Ashtanga Yoga system
Pratyahara	("withdrawal"): principles of self-control; the fifth limb of Patanjali's Ashtanga Yoga system
Pratipaksha bhavana	overcoming negative feelings with positive ones
Purusha	the indwelling Self: the Absolute Spirit, Brahman; the conductor of the life-force of every human being
Rajas/rajasic	one of the three qualities of nature (*guna*), expressing extreme activity and restlessness; derived from the root *raj/ranj*, "to be colored" or "to be excited, charmed"
Rishi	("seer"): seer or sage; person of right vision and action
Sa	the real doer, the soul
Sadhana	("means of realization"): spiritual practice

Sahasrara chakra	("thousand-spoked wheel"): the chakra located at the top of the head in the fontanel; crown of the head
Sadanga Yoga	the yoga of six limbs
Samadhi	state of communion with God; merged and engrossed in God consciousness; realization; superconscious state; complete freedom from nature's three *gunas*; the eighth and last limb of Patanjali's Ashtanga Yoga system
Samkhya	(school of philosophy): the path of knowledge
Sannyasa ashrama	life of renunciation for Self-realization
Sarira parigraha	out of ignorance, the acceptance of the body as the self
Santosha	contentment
Sattva/sattvic	one of the three qualities of nature (*guna*), expressing calmness and spirituality
Satya loka	the seventh of the seven upper spheres of existence (*loka*); corresponds to the fontanel (God center); plane of experiencing truth

Satyam	truth
Satya pratistha	to be established in truth
Shambhavi mudra	an open-eyed meditation technique to perceive the divine light
Shastras	ancient Indian holy scriptures
Shaucha	purity
Shesha	the mythological snake on which Lord Vishnu (the sustainer of creation) of the Hindu trinity rests
Siddhi	("accomplishment"): perfection and revelation; namely, attaining the state of *nirvikalpa samadhi*, becoming merged in God and God consciousness
Sutra	thread or link; aphorisms, as in Patanjali's Yoga Sutra
Svadhisthana chakra	("wheel of the Self (*sva*) base (*adhishthana*)"): the lumbar (procreation) center
Svadhyaya	comes from *sva* (soul) plus *adhyaya* (culture or study); to study one's own self is soul culture
Svah loka	the third of the seven upper spheres of existence (*loka*). Corresponds to the food (fire) center; plane of brilliance

Tamas/tamasic	one of the three qualities of nature (*guna*), expressing sloth and idleness
Tanmatras	the five subtle elements: the five sense objects consisting of objects of sight, hearing, smell, taste, and touch
Tapah loka	the sixth of the seven upper spheres of existence (*loka*). Corresponds to the pituitary (soul center); plane of meditation
Tapas	ordinarily this means doing penance and austerities, but the metaphorical meaning is to watch the breath as an oblation in the holy fire that maintains the heat in the body. *Tapas* means that in every breath one loves God and remains alert.
Tapasvi	those who perform austerities and penance
Tryang Yoga	three-limbed yoga: *tapah* (austerity or observing the breath as the oblation in the holy fire in the cranium), *svadhyaya* (study of the scriptures or the study of one's self), and *ishwara*

	pranidhani (surrender to God or cultivating the path of devotion) is known as Kriya Yoga
Vaksiddhi	*siddhi* attained by a person who speaks truth all the time, which means that whatever comes out of the mouth of such a person comes true
Vanaprastha ashrama	the life of retirement (to the forest) for selfless service
Vasana kshaya	*vasana* ("desires") and *kshaya* ("to destroy"): the elimination of unnecessary desires
Virya	strength, vitality, vigor, and valor
Vishuddha chakra	("pure wheel"): the cervical, throat, or religion center
Yajna	("sacrifice") oblation in fire; sacrifice. The breath is constantly offered as an oblation to the soul fire in the cave of the cranium. In a broader sense, every activity of every living being that is in the form of enjoying sense objects, is sacrifice (*yajna*).
Yama	ethical living: self-discipline, restraint; the first limb of

	Patanjali's Ashtanga Yoga system, which includes nonviolence, truthfulness, non-stealing, celibacy, and non-possessiveness
Yoga	("yoking") a branch of Indian philosophy; esoteric meditation; to perceive the constant union with the divine Self in every breath, in every moment, in every activity, and in every achievement. Yoga is the way you can perceive divinity manifested in the whole universe as well as in the entire body.
Yogastha	the state of the body and soul joined together and performing all the actions
Yoga Sutra	aphorisms on yoga as described by Sage Patanjali

About the Author

Paramahamsa Prajnanananda is the current spiritual leader of the Kriya Yoga international organizations. These organizations were founded by his master, Paramahamsa Hariharananda, who spread the teachings of Kriya Yoga all over the world. Paramahamsa Hariharananda was Swami Shriyukteshwar and Paramahamsa Yogananda's most outstanding direct disciple, one of the greatest realized Kriya Yoga masters in the lineage of Mahavatar Babaji Maharaj and Lahiri Mahasaya.

Born in Orissa, Paramahamsa Prajnanananda was raised in a profound spiritual environment that inspired his search for Truth. He received his higher education in Cuttack and became a professor of economics there. In 1980, while still a student, he met Paramahamsa Hariharananda, who initiated him into Kriya Yoga, then fifteen years later, into the sacred path of *sannyas.* After only three years, at the early age of 39, his master conferred upon him the highest title of Paramahamsa, a designation reserved for monks and saints who have attained the summit of realization.

Enriched by his own direct experience, fathomless wisdom, and deep love for humanity, Paramahamsa Prajnanananda guides and inspires spiritual seekers, a living example of how to fulfill one's infinite potential. In addition to running the main ashrams in Puri, Cuttack, Vienna, and Miami, Prajnananandaji spreads spiritual knowledge and the ancient science of Kriya Yoga by holding seminars and retreats all over the world. Prajnana Mission, founded by Paramahamsa Prajnanananda, provides service to humanity with free medical assistance units and centers, residential schools for the poor, and many other charitable and educational activities.

Author of many books on the science of yoga, practical guidelines to the application of the wisdom of Vedantic philosophy, and insightful metaphorical commentaries on the major holy scriptures and world religions, Paramahamsa Prajnanananda binds and bridges Eastern and Western cultures with a harmonious, fresh, and non-sectarian approach.

Kriya Yoga

The ancient history of Kriya Yoga is mystifying and mesmerizing. Its mysterious origins are an intermingling of mythology, history, and science that date from the dawn of human consciousness. Saints and sages of India have long practiced and spread the science of yoga. Kriya Yoga is a very ancient and effective yogic science as well as an age-old tradition that has been practiced by seers, saints, and sages since time immemorial.

In Indian mythology, even Rama and Krishna practiced and taught the Kriya meditation technique. Kriya practices were explained by the rishis in the Upanishads, by Sage Vasishtha in Yoga Vasishtha, and by Maharshi Patañjali in his Yoga Sutra.

The Bhagavad Gita (4:1) says that God first revealed the Kriya technique to Vivashvan, then Vivashvan passed it to his son Manu, the seventh of the fourteen Manus or progenitors of the human race. Manu then transmitted it to his son Ikshvaku, founder of the first dynasty of kings in ancient India. From then on this technique was transmitted from father to son, which metaphorically means from master to disciple, through direct oral transmission. Apparently lost in the increasing spiritual decline of later epochs, these teachings were revived by the timeless Mahavatar Babaji Maharaj in 1861, who named the technique "Kriya Yoga."

Available Books on Yoga, Philosophy and Spirituality

by Swami Satyananda Giri
Yogananda Sanga, ISBN 3-902038-22-5

by Paramahamsa Hariharananda
Kriya Yoga: The Scientific Process of Soul Culture and the Essence of all Religions, ISBN 81-86713-05-0
Each Human Body is a Bhagavad Gita,ISBN 81-87825-06-5
Bhagavad Gita in the Light of Kriya Yoga,
Volume I: ISBN 0-9639107-0-1, Volume II: ISBN 0-9639107-1-X, Volume III: ISBN 0-9639107-2-8
Bhagavad Gita Pocket Book, ISBN 978-3-87823-45-6
Divine Quest, ISBN 978-3-902038-77-2
Isha Upanishad, ISBN 85-081923
Mysticism of Religious Symbols, ISBN 3-902038-66-7
Nectar Drops (2nd Edition), ISBN 978-3-902038-68-5
Ocean of Divine Bliss: The Complete Works of Kriya Yoga Master Paramahamsa Hariharananda (10 volumes) PB 978-3-902038-41-8, HB 978-3-902038-51-7
Humble Hariharananda, Letters and Messages
ISBN 978-902038-72-2
Songs of the Mystics, ISBN 978-3-902038-71-5
Spirit of Religions, ISBN 978-3-902038-73-9
Words of Wisdom, Inspiring Stories and Parables (2nd Edition)
ISBN 978-3-902038-70-8

by Paramahamsa Prajnanananda
Mahavatar Babaji: The Eternal Light of God (2nd Edition)
ISBN 3-902038-28-4
Lahiri Mahasaya: Fountainhead of Kriya Yoga (2nd Edition)
ISBN 978-3-99000-007-6
Swami Shriyukteshwar: Incarnation of Wisdom,
ISBN 3-901665-23-4
The Lineage of Kriya Yoga Masters, ISBN 3-902038-13-6
My Time with the Master, ISBN 3-902038-08-X
Discourses on the Bhagavad Gita, Volume I, ISBN 3-901665-25-0, Volume II, ISBN 3-901665-26-9

The Universe Within, ISBN 3-902038-14-4
Yoga, Pathway of the Divine (3rd Edition) ISBN 3-99000-004-5
The Path of Love, ISBN 3-902038-07-1
Life and Values, ISBN 3-902038-09-8
Akshara Tattva, ISBN 81-87825-02-2
Nava Durga: The Multiple Forms of the Mother, ISBN 3-901665-28-5
Krishna Katha, ISBN 1-931733-00-7
A Successful Lifestyle, ISBN 1-931733-03-1
Daily Prayers, ISBN 1-931733-02-3
The Changing Nature of Relationships, ISBN 3-902038-10-1
Prapanna Gita, ISBN 1-971733-01-5
Daily Reflections, ISBN 3-
Kriya Yoga: Path of Soul Culture, ISBN 81-87825-07-3
Gautama Buddha, (2nd Edition) ISBN 978-3-99000-001-4 (PB) 978-3-99000-006-9 (HB)
The Body's Dance, the Soul's Play, ISBN 3-902038-17-9
Jnana Sankalini Tantra, PB ISBN 3-902038-18-7, HB 3-902038 20-9
Rama Katha, ISBN 3-902038-23-2
The Last Decade, A Loving Recollection, ISBN 3-902038-24-1
River of Compassion: The Life of Paramahamsa Hariharananda, (2nd Edition) ISBN 3-902038-27-6
The Torah, the Bible and Kriya Yoga: Metaphorical Explanation of the Torah and the New Testament in the Light of Kriya Yoga (2nd Edition) ISBN 978-3-902038-29-6
My Brother, Brahmanandaji, ISBN 978-3-902038-69-2

Other Books about Paramahamsa Hariharananda

Life and Teachings of Paramahamsa Hariharananda ISBN 3-902038-30-6
In Memoriam (2nd Edition) ISBN 3-902038-31-4
Kriya Yoga: In the I ›w of Omniscience ISBN 978-902038-65-4
Footprints of the Master, Memories of Baba Hariharananda ISBN 978-902038-74-6

Children's Literature Series

Paramahamsa Hariharananda - A Yogi of Modern India, ISBN 978-3-902038-76-0

Books by other authors

You Are What You Eat, by Sandra Heber - Percy ISBN 978-3-902038-78-4

Kriya Yoga Contacts

Kriya Yoga Centre Vienna

Pottendorferstrasse 69 A-2523 Tattendorf Austria
Tel: 43 2253 81491 Fax: 43 2253 80462
E-mail: kriya.yoga.centre@aon.at
Web: www.kriyayoga-europe.org

Hariharananda Gurukulam

P.O. Chaitana, Balighai, Puri 750002, Orissa, India
Tel/Fax: 0091 6752 246644
E-mail: missionprajnana@gmail.com
Web: www.prajnanamission.org

Kriya Yoga Contacts

Kriya Yoga Institute

P.O. Box 924615 Homestead,
FL 33092-4615 USA
Tel: 1 305 247 1960 Fax: 1 305 248 1951
E-mail: institute@kriya.org Web: www.kriya.org

Kriya Yoga Centrum

Heezerweg 7, Sterksel, NL-6029 PP, Holland
Tel: 31 40 2265576
Fax: 31 40 2265612
E-mail: kriya.yoga@worldonline.nl